D1459728

HORIZON

SPRING, 1972 · VOLUME XIV, NUMBER 2

⊂HORIZON

SPRING, 1972 · VOLUME XIV, NUMBER 2

EDITOR IN CHIEF
Joseph J. Thorndike

EDITOR
Charles L. Mee, Jr.
MANAGING EDITOR: Robert Cowley
ART EDITOR: Jane Wilson
ART DIRECTOR: Kenneth Munowitz
ASSOCIATE EDITORS: Shirley Tomkievicz, Ormonde de Kay, Jr.
CONTRIBUTING EDITORS: Walter Karp, Barbara Klaw
ASSISTANT EDITOR: Mary Sherman Parsons
EDITORIAL ASSISTANTS: W. Jeffrey Simpson, Susan G. Ferris
COPY EDITOR: Mary Ann Pfeiffer
ASSISTANT COPY EDITOR: Kaethe Ellis
ASSISTANT TO THE EDITOR: J. Muriel Vrotsos
ROVING EDITOR: Frederic V. Grunfeld

ADVISORY BOARD
Gilbert Highet, *Chairman,* Frederick Burkhardt,
William Harlan Hale, John Walker
EUROPEAN CONSULTING EDITOR: J. H. Plumb, *Christ's College, Cambridge*
CHIEF, EUROPEAN BUREAU: Gertrudis Feliu, *11 rue du Bouloi, Paris 1ᵉʳ*

AMERICAN HERITAGE PUBLISHING COMPANY
PRESIDENT AND PUBLISHER
Paul Gottlieb

EDITORIAL ART DIRECTOR
Murray Belsky

SENIOR EDITORS, HORIZON
Marshall B. Davidson
Oliver Jensen

HORIZON is published every three months by American Heritage Publishing Co., Inc. Editorial and executive offices: 551 Fifth Avenue, New York, N.Y. 10017. Treasurer: Marjorie C. Dyer. Secretary: John C. Taylor 3rd. All correspondence about subscriptions should be addressed to: HORIZON Subscription Office, 379 West Center St., Marion, Ohio 43302.

Single copies: $6.00. Subscriptions: $20.00 per year in the U.S. and Canada; elsewhere, $21.00.

Cumulative indexes for Volumes I–V and VI–X are available at $3. HORIZON is also indexed in the *Readers' Guide to Periodical Literature.* The editors welcome contributions but can assume no responsibility for un-solicited material. Title registered U.S. Patent Office. Second-class postage paid at New York, N.Y., and at additional mailing offices.

Changeless History?

Nothing remains the same, proclaimed the ancien[t] Greek philosopher Heraclitus. Nothing really change[s] said the ancient Greek philosopher Parmenides. "[O] *tempora! O mores!*" the Roman elder sighed, be[-] moaning the alteration in things familiar and dea[r.] "*Plus ça change, plus c'est la même chose,*" the Pari[-] sian wit shrugs, mocking the mongers of illusionar[y] novelties.

This ageless and unresolved philosophical deba[te] has not left HORIZON magazine untouched. In rece[nt] years we editors, too, have found ourselves divide[d] along the ancient lines of battle: between the *O-tem[-] porists,* so to speak, and the *Plus-ça-changists.* Speci[f-] ically, the debate has been joined among us over th[e] following inescapable question: does the past real[ly] provide useful and illuminating parallels to the pre[s-] ent condition of man and society? Or, *per contra,* ha[ve] we entered an entirely new era (whether new daw[n] or new dark age being, in logic at any rate, a secon[d-] ary question) that makes most historical paralle[ls] misleading? To put it another way, do we study hi[s-] tory for signs of change, or do we study it for signs [of] permanence?

In the latest issue of HORIZON the *Plus-ça-chang[e]* faction has temporarily gained the upper hand. Th[e] opening cluster of essays on spring, for example, [is] based quite explicitly on the proposition that what[-] ever else has happened to humankind, the round [of] the seasons and man's essential response to it, ha[ve] not changed at all. There also appears in this issue [a] fairly neat historical parallel between the career [of] the mystical sage Gurdjieff, who flourished won[-] drously after World War I—his story is told b[y] Kenneth Cavander in an article beginning on pag[e] 58—and the present-day "gurus" of California— photographed for HORIZON by Anthony Ray-Jon[es] —who have risen *de novo* in yet another trouble[d] time.

Lionel Casson's description of ancient voyage[s,] which begins on page 96, provides a veritable com[-] pendium of yet another sort of persistence: the pe[r-] sistence of certain leading ideas, regardless of factu[al] evidence. In Mr. Casson's account, the chief idea [in] question is the belief that, for a given ocean, the[re] must have existed some man or tribe who crossed [it] long before the heroes accredited in official historie[s.] On the basis of that indomitable faith, the civilizin[g] f the New World has been attributed to Pacific-crossing Chinese, Indians, Polynesians and the inhabitants of fabled Mu; to Atlantic-crossing Israelies, Phoenicians, Egyptians, and the residents of faled Atlantis. As Mr. Casson makes clear, every time ne such hypothetical voyage is sunk by the evidence, nother one bobs up in its place. (The great voyages of hor Heyerdahl, described in an article beginning on age 104, have recently provided a good deal of impetus for fresh argument.) What persists unchanged the hypothesis itself—a sort of *idée fixe* of the uman mind.

The more stubborn adherents of the no-change rinciple can draw comfort as well from J. H. Plumb's ccount of that immortal aristocratic gossip, the Duc e Saint-Simon, chronicler of the days and ways of he court of Louis the Sun King. The titled courtiers f Versailles have long since fled—have long since een driven, in fact—from the stage of history, but ourts and courtiers have not, since they arise almost utomatically in every select circle surrounding men f great power. When the United States entered /orld War II, British diplomats and military atiches asked D. W. Brogan what books they might ead as a guide to Washington and the White House. aint-Simon's diaries, replied the great British student of American politics. The White House, he explained, resembled nothing so much as a royal court. *lus ça change,* you might say.

The great debate, however, is not so readily resolved, for each time a new topic comes up for discussion, the factions regroup. When some bizarre nd unsettling new art mode makes its appearance, or example, the issue is instantly joined: do we emhasize, perhaps, the fact that most new art modes oked bizarre and ugly to contemporaries, including npressionist paintings, now so familiar and loved? r, on the other hand, do we incline to view the new henomenon as the latest stage in the erosion of a ng tradition of art—an erosion that began, possily, with those very same impressionists? Again, do e disturbing antics of modern-day youth, or the gns of the dissolution of the family, derive from ome truly new condition of life? Or should we, ther, look on them as the temporary symptoms of temporary social breakdown of the sort humannd has undergone—and repaired—time and again the past? Heraclitus and Parmenides keep tugging way. W.K.

COVER: A maiden symbolizing spring strolls through a meadow picking blossoms in a Roman fresco painted around the first century B.C. Her back turned to the viewer, she appears as gracefully indifferent to us as she is to the robe that has slipped from her shoulder. The fresco was recovered from a house that was buried by Vesuvius at Stabiae in A.D. 79.
MUSEO NAZIONALE, NAPLES—SCALA

THE RITES OF SPRING

Twenty-five hundred years ago this spring, Greek maidens were dancing wildly on Mount Parnassus to honor the great god Dionysus. Four thousand years ago this spring, Babylonians were taking part in mock battles and stripping their king of his official regalia. These were the magical rites of spring, carried out to ensure the renewal of the earth's fertility, the celebrations of ancient people steeped in superstition. Or so, at any rate, it once seemed. When Sir James Frazer published *The Golden Bough* in 1890, his Victorian readers confidently concluded that modern man in his marvelous progress had laid aside such childish toys. Today we are not so certain that ancient festivals were quite so childlike or that the need for seasonal rituals was merely the province of myth-ridden barbarians. Despite the vast changes wrought by history, the seasons themselves have not changed, and modern man still shares with his ancient forebears the same environment of the calendar: the annual waxing and waning of daylight; the longest day, about June 22; the longest night, about December 22; the breakup of winter's frigid routines; the lifting of summertime torpor. In our response to the unchanging seasons lies a common bond between us and our ancestors and the common bond among ourselves.

The psychology of the seasons is still an obscure subject, but common experience indicates its salient principle: at certain junctures of the year there arises among men a general fever of the blood, a sort of common malaise, a complex yearning for something outside the ordinary round of life. Men can give it public form and expression or, if they choose, can ignore it. The calendrical malaise, however, is inextinguishable; it returns each year with the moment that excites it.

The cruelest month? The rites of spring resemble Sadie Hawkins Day in James Thurber's cover for The New Yorker *of April 27, 1940. Above, Picasso's flowery gift celebrates the season in gentler fashion.*

Take, for example, the juncture known as the winter solstice, the moment when the shrinking day has shrunk to its smallest and will begin once again to roll back the night. It is at one and the same time the mark of winter's onset and the distant harbinger of summer light. Pagan Rome gave expression to the complex emotions it arouses in a holiday known as the Saturnalia, a week of general license in which schools were closed, declarations of war forbidden, and distinctions of rank momentarily discarded. Roman paganism died out, but the winter solstice did not; the early Christians located the celebration of Christ's nativity at the same place in the year. The religious change involved was, of course, enormous, but the underlying passion of the solstice has remained. Indeed, it appears to be a "Saturnalian" one, as Christian moralists have had cause to complain throughout the Christian Era. We see its force today in the annual frenzy of Christmas shopping, a sort of Saturnalian release appropriate to a society of consumers. We see its expression in the annual office Christmas party, which, like the pagan Saturnalia, is an occasion for ignoring distinctions of rank. One way or another the urge of a season finds its outlet.

But it is spring that arouses in us the strongest, most insistent, and most complex of all seasonal emotions. On the following pages we have tried to exhibit something of its singular force and variety—in the Dionysian rites of ancient Greece, in the twisted career of a single spring holiday, May Day; as a phenomenon of biology, as an event in the history of modern music, as the subject for one of the most remarkable of paintings. The essay on *The Golden Bough* shows how the central theme of spring—the annual renewal of life—runs like a bright thread through an enormous tapestry of ancient rites and enduring myths. Mankind has never failed to respond to that annual renewal of life. It arises within us as the fever in the blood known as spring.   W.K.

In a lush baroque glen, plump putti *and handmaidens attend Flora, the ancient goddess of Spring.* Flora in a Garden *was painted by Jan Brueg*

68–1625). Symbol of springtime joy, the lovely Flora first appeared in Western art in Botticelli's Primavera, *painted in the fifteenth century*

Spring's Alarm Clocks

From monarch butterfly to man, the season goes off inside us, like a ringing in the blood

After the long winter, a magic day arrives. Overnight the air has lost its chill. A balminess lifts our spirits, leaves unfurl, and the air carries the fragrance of new growth. A frog croaks a tentative note, another answers, and a noisy counterpoint rises along the edge of the pond. Overhead, geese wing northward in V formation.

Man has always associated the burgeoning of spring with the coming of warmer weather; the spring warmth, we feel, has roused the earth from dormancy. But this assumption now appears to be mostly wrong. Within the past fifty years, science has shown that factors other than rising temperatures are responsible for the sprouting of seeds, the flowering of plants, the eclosion of insects, the spring migration of birds, the rousing of animals from hibernation—or the turning of a young man's fancy. But even without the scientific experiments that proved this to be so, a keener observation of nature could have led us to question whether warmer days were the only cause of the spring displays.

It has long been known, for example, that the arctic tern winters on the Cape of Good Hope, and when spring approaches, flies northwest across the Atlantic to breeding grounds within the Arctic Circle. But the Cape of Good Hope lies far south of the equator, and when the urge for spring migration overtakes the tern, it is fall in South Africa and the days are getting cooler, not warmer. (The days are also getting shorter, and day-length is a critical factor in the recognition of the seasons, as we shall see.)

Again, the palolo worm of Fijian seas stages an annual "rising" when it is spring in the South Pacific. William Burrows reports that this polychaete worm lives in the coral reefs and, with the approach of November, the hind part of the worm swells with sex cells. During the last quarter of the moon, in October or November, these hind parts free themselves from the head, surge to the surface of the sea, and break up to release eggs and sperm. Rising temperatures can hardly cause this, for the air temperatures in Fiji are quite uniform, and the ocean temperatures are even more so.

*A*nother spring display that does not appear to be initiated by rising temperatures is that of the monarch butterfly, whose beautiful orange wings, edged and veined in black, are known throughout the United States. The most publicized of the monarch's five migration routes up and down the continent extends from Canada to the butterfly trees in Pacific Grove, California. Do rising temperatures in Pacific Grove tell the monarch when it is time to wing to Canada? It seems most unlikely. The Monterey peninsula faces the Pacific, and the cooling effects of the Japan Current on the water and the ocean fogs on the air prevent any significant temperature rise. Moreover, the time of spring migration varies from late February to late March, so to assign some temperature level as the cause of the spring flight would strain the facts.

Scientists began to suspect that some other process was at work in the biological rites of spring as early as 1918. That year, Wightman Garner and Harry Allard, of the U.S. Department of Agriculture, set out to find a way of obtaining seeds from field crops of an outstanding new variety of tobacco, the Maryland Mammouth. The Mammouth was commercially choice; it grew to a height of ten or fifteen feet and produced as many as a hundred leaves on a single plant. But it also had a serious fault. It would not set seed in the field until so late in the fall that frost killed the plants.

In their first experiments, Garner and Allard grew their plants at higher temperatures, expecting to induce earlier flowering. This didn't work. Trial after trial involving other seasonal variables also failed. Indeed, Garner at last wrote, "the problem [then] appeared to assume a somewhat hopeless trend . . ." But finally, "after much deliberation it was concluded that the only remaining seasonal phenomenon that could be a factor was change in the relative length of the day and night." With this clue, the two scientists soon found that it *was* the length of the day that governed flowering. By sheltering experimental plants in a dark house for part of the long summer daylight, they induced their experimental plants to flower in twenty-six days, while control plants in the open field required one hundred and ten

By RITCHIE WARD

days. The phenomenon was termed "photoperiodism," and the duration of daylight was referred to as the "photoperiod."

Far more remarkable than the discovery itself was what it implied: that a plant can measure a period of time! This opened floodgates of new research in biology. More and more investigators took up studies that were to lead to the concept of "living clocks." Within the past twenty-five years these studies have shown that living organisms ranging from one-celled plants to man can measure time, and can do so with amazing precision.

At mid-century a German scientist, Gustav Kramer, discovered that starlings pinpoint the goals of their spring and fall migrations through their ability to navigate by the sun. About the same time, another German, the great Karl von Frisch, showed that honeybees also navigate by the sun. Of course, navigation cannot be accomplished solely by fixing the position of a celestial body. The navigator also has to know the exact time. Kramer's starlings and Von Frisch's bees must therefore be equipped with extremely accurate internal clocks.

To be this accurate, the clocks would surely have to be temperature-compensated. Two hundred years ago, a ship's longitude could be determined only roughly, for temperature changes might cause the navigator's chronometer to gain or lose up to five minutes a day. Nowadays, with compensated balance wheels that run true over wide ranges of temperature, and balance springs of Invar or Elinvar, chronometers keep within a second a day of the exact time. Similarly, the clocks of plants, animals, and men are essentially unaffected by temperature changes, as a convincing body of experimental evidence now demonstrates.

We know, then, that living organisms measure time by referring to accurate, temperature-compensated internal clocks. But what other variables in the environment might affect the clocks? Does the diurnal shift from day to night have any particular influence?

Consider the flying squirrel, who sleeps through the day in his den tree in Wisconsin and then—within a minute or two of dusk—rouses, glides from the den tree, and begins a round of nocturnal activity. What triggers the awakening? Patricia DeCoursey, in an experiment with flying squirrels, kept them for many days in the laboratory, at a constant temperature and in continuous light: her animals still slept when it was daytime outside and became active at dusk. So something more than the visible arrival of dusk tells the flying squirrel when it is time to stir. This must be his internal clock.

*J*ust how he reads his internal clock remains a mystery. Probably it is related to his critical photoperiod. Donald Farner, Michael Menaker, and other experimenters have demonstrated that many animals show photoperiodic responses. These include such diverse species as mites, potato beetles, corn borers, the three-spined stickleback, ferrets, white-crowned sparrows, and the varying hare.

In spite of all their mysteries, we know enough about living clocks to ask how an organism could use a daily cycle to perceive an annual event such as the coming of spring. We have already suggested one way: an organism might use its clock to measure the length of the day, and upon receiving the information that a day long enough to be a spring day had arrived, it would "know" that spring had come. A different mechanism has been suggested by Frank Brown, Jr. He speculates that organisms may have a way of counting daily cycles, perhaps as a computer scans a tape, and after 365 cycles have run past a scanner, an action switch goes on.

On the other hand, some evidence favors a true annual rhythm quite independent of the daily clock. Eric Pengelley and the late Kenneth Fisher kept golden-mantled ground squirrels, which are typical hibernators, in a windowless room lighted artificially for twelve hours a day. A continuous supply of food and water was maintained, and the temperature was held constant at 72 degrees. In the wilds of their own high Rocky Mountains, these animals do not hibernate until the temperature drops to close to freezing, but in the constant higher temperature of the laboratory they still alternated hibernation and activity in their regular seasons. They responded to spring without a single direct clue.

Many other annual rhythms have been observed, but not many have been carefully studied. The time needed to collect a significant body of data is discouraging, for one must wait a year between observations.

Naturally, we would like to know as much as we can about our own annual rhythms, but man is a notoriously poor experimental animal. He finds it amusing to bend his IBM card and ruin an experiment; what's more, his responses tend to depart from patterns. Our own clocks are the least well understood of those that have been studied.

Biologists agree that the behavior of living forms has evolved to give the individual his best chance of survival. Seeds do not sprout, birds do not mate, bears do not fare forth, until the danger of killing cold has passed. The first robins do not appear before earthworms come to the surface of the ground. Honeybees wait for spring pollen, swallows wait for insects on the wing, hummingbirds migrate in the wake of nectar-bearing flowers. Each of our well-loved signs of spring has its place in the great ecological pattern.

But there is yet a deeper mystery. The physiological preparations for spring begin well in advance. The gonads of birds and mammals start to swell months before the first spring day, and how the internal clock initiates the process is not known. Mystery still compounds mystery.

Ritchie Ward, who lives in California, wrote The Living Clocks, *published last year by Knopf. It is a popular account of the mysteries of biological timing.*

THE DIONYSIAN FRENZY

Only if you lose yourself can you find yourself:
such is the message of the eternal orgy of spring

As the action of *Bacchae*, one of the last plays by the Greek playwright Euripides, moves toward its climax, the attention of the audience is focused on the story of a young man last seen dressed in women's clothing. Quivering with anticipation, he sits on the limb of a pine tree overlooking a little valley; from its branches he expects to look out on a crowd of women, men, and beasts plunged in erotic oblivion, performing acts he has only been able to imagine in his most obscene fantasies. But perched in his tree, the young man, whose name is Pentheus, is disappointed: he can see nothing.

Then, from the ground below, comes a hideous, half-human shriek. He recognizes the distorted voice: his own mother is one of the women he has come to spy on. Her voice is joined by a chorus of other females. They scream frantically; they want to kill him. Pentheus is terrified.

This scene, written nearly 2,400 years ago, is about to explode into one of the most grotesque and horrific climaxes in the history of drama. Yet the story Euripides tells is hallowed by centuries of ritual and tradition. It is the basis for springtime cults all over ancient Greece. It is the story of Dionysus.

The god, superhuman power, force of nature—call him what you like—known to ancient Greece as Dionysus was an interloper in the serene band of Olympians. Although Zeus and Hera, Apollo, Aphrodite, Hermes, and the rest of the immortals had recognizably human passions and failings, there was always something respectable about them. They had impeccably nonhuman pedigrees going back to such comfortable abstractions as Time, Darkness, and Chaos. Dionysus broke into the club like a *nouveau riche* cad.

In the first place, he came late. Homer, the earliest surviving authority on the Olympian hierarchy, mentions him as an ominous figure stirring up trouble in Thrace, a wild and barbarous country to the north of Greece. Worse still, Dionysus was only half divine. Zeus, in one of his many unions with mortals, slept with the daughter of King Cadmus of Thebes, Semele. Most of Zeus's "illegitimate" children became heroes or demigods, but the child of Zeus and Semele became Dionysus, the god of wine, who could tame snakes, make the earth spout milk and honey, and force mothers to tear their sons limb from limb.

Dionysus was a worker of miracles, but the greatest miracle of all was his

Joined by a reveling band of satyrs and maenads, Bacchus—as Dionysus was known by the Romans—leaps from his chariot to greet Ariadne, at left, in Titian's Bacchus and Ariadne *(circa 1520). The figure entwined by the snake is the wine god's tutor, Silenus.*

10   *By* KENNETH CAVANDER

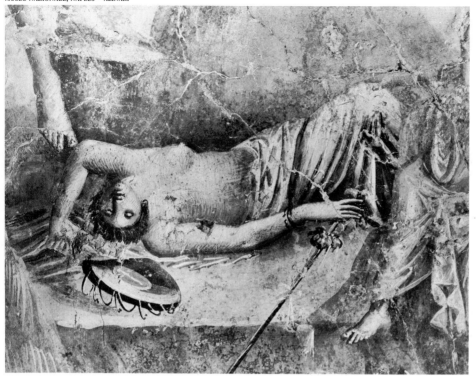

First century: a Dionysian celebrant lies contorted in sleep in this wall painting from Pompeii.

survival. When Semele found she was with child, she prayed to see the child's father face to face. Zeus warned her that it was dangerous. Semele insisted. Zeus granted her prayer, and the pregnant Semele was incinerated along with her bridal chamber in a blast of lightning. But Dionysus lived. Zeus snatched him out of his mother's womb and carried him to Olympus, where he spent the rest of his prenatal life in Zeus's thigh.

Thus the Greeks came to speak of Dionysus as "twice-born"—once from his mother, a second time from his father. It seems plausible that what the village storytellers who circulated the legend meant was that Dionysus found temporary shelter not in Zeus's thigh but in his genital sac.

For Dionysus, his second birth was to be delivered from his father's loins; for mankind, a second birth is a mystic regeneration of the self; for nature, it is the simple fact of spring. The festivals of Dionysus span the months from December to mid-March. In December the harvest lies locked in barns; the seeds are stored in the frozen earth; the grape juice is bottled. But the dead of winter is very much alive. Under the snow the seeds put down green shoots; the wine ferments. The earth is at work in its sleep. The force that keeps it alive and

shakes it into green wakefulness in the spring is Dionysus.

To aid him in his task, Zeus gave Dionysus a train of followers, called "maenads," or "bacchae." They were usually women; they played flutes, pounded on drums and tambourines, and danced—they danced tirelessly. Maenads wore the delicate skins of young deer; in their hands they carried pine branches and ivy leaves—evergreens defying winter—and snakes coiled in their hair. In the spring they drank the new wine, the blood-red juice of Dionysus that makes men mad. Sometimes Dionysus himself appeared as a bull god, crowned with horns; the bull and goat, with their unflagging phallic power, were his sacrificial beasts.

*W*hen he arrived in a new place, though, this bringer of ecstasy and regeneration was not always welcome. At first this seems strange: who could reject the coming of new life? But the legends that record the hostile reception Dionysus got in city after city of mythical Greece reflect a profound mystery —the inextricable unity of life and death.

Just as the sexual act is at the same time life-giving and death-seeming—a *petite mort,* as the French express it—

so in order to be reborn you must first die. Only if you lose yourself can you find yourself. This is the message of the Mysteries and the secret of all initiation. It is the secret of nature herself: the seed dies in the soil to be reborn as a plant. To the critical intellect such paradoxes are nothing but irritating contradictions. But Dionysus came into the world to abolish all contradictions. In his orgies (the Greek word *orgia* means sacred rites) the individual is submerged in the mass like a drop of water in the ocean; it is no accident that the songs—or were they howls of ecstasy? —of his original worshipers became in time the choral odes of that most collective of the arts, the theatre.

So Dionysus's harsh welcome is explained. He comes like a revolution, a psychic insurrection, laying reason to sleep with wine and annihilating the comfortable everyday self. To the man who is not at one with nature, that is, to any "civilized" man, the death of his mundane self and the awakening of a teeming, unruly, autonomous life-force within him is bound to be threatening. His precious ego is at stake. And look at Dionysus himself. In the imagination of most of those who have known him—artists, seers, poets, madmen— he is young and good-looking, but it is hard to tell his gender; his skin is soft and his limbs pliant, like a woman's; he wears flowing robes and long hair, yet he is man enough to create a hysteria of sexual delirium among women wherever he goes. No wonder all good citizens, all solid and sensible folk, confronted with this sexually ambiguous demon, turn him away as an intruder and a subversive.

For this defiance Dionysus exacts a terrible vengeance. The roll call is ominous: Lycurgus, king of Thrace, blinded, driven mad, pulled apart by horses; the women of the city of Argos frenzied and driven to kill their own children; the women of Boeotia plagued by hallucinations, seeing their looms turn into vines; the crew of a pirate ship, unwittingly taking him on board, turned into dolphins; and the women of Thebes running crazed to the mountainsides with their queen, Agave, while Pentheus, her son, who has tried and failed to imprison the revelers, is persuaded to don women's clothing and go to the place where the women are dancing to spy on their rituals.

*I*n the scene from Euripides' play, *Bacchae*, with which we began, Pentheus is perched on his pine branch, while at the foot of the tree is a throng of frenzied maenads, among them his own mother. By one of those miracles that abound in the legends about Dionysus, the women seize the tree and uproot it with their bare hands. They pounce on the king and, with his mother leading them, tear him limb from limb. When he is dead, they play catch with gobbets of his flesh.

So Pentheus, dressed as a woman, becomes an eerie double of the bisexual Dionysus, who, as it happens, is also his cousin. In the earliest versions of the legend, it is Dionysus who is torn apart. But Euripides makes Pentheus his stand-in for the climactic scene of dismemberment. Once every two years, in historical times, the women of Greece would leave their homes on a certain night in mid-winter, go to the mountains, and dance in the snow, dressed in fawn-skins, possessed. There was no drinking, for this was winter, but at the climax of the ceremony an animal, it might be a goat or a bull, was torn apart; then the women ate its bleeding flesh still warm, sharing in communion the raw power of Dionysus himself.

Ancient Athens tamed these violent ceremonies. There were three Athenian festivals associated with Dionysus: the Rural Dionysia, in December, in which a cake and a phallic symbol were consecrated to the god; later, toward the middle of January, the Lenaea, with plays and processions; and finally, in mid-March, the most lavish of all—the Greater Dionysia, a city-wide festival with displays of wealth and power and the performances of tragedy and comedy that made the theatre of Dionysus at Athens famous.

Twentieth century: a protester collapses following the frenzy of a springtime antiwar march.

But if the action of the ritual became civilized and cultivated, the spirit of the myth did not. In the spring, wine bottled the previous year was opened, and spread its message of disorder and madness through the veins of the holidaymakers. Generations of children were fathered in those nights of Dionysian chaos, in thickets and shadows outside some Greek city.

Meanwhile, other gods with other titles absorbed the wildness of Dionysus. They were, like him, foreigners, newcomers with exotic names like Sabazios, Bendis, and Adonis, who invaded Greek culture at the end of the fifth century B.C. When the Romans came and took over Greece, Dionysus simply went underground and was reincarnated as a multitude of Roman and Near Eastern cult figures.

And he lives still. Just as the sexual license of the ancient Dionysian festivals abolished all distinctions and annihilated the boundaries of the self, so today's bliss seekers search for nirvana in a capsule and, by annihilating all rational structures, hope to let the green shoots of a new consciousness peek through the cracks. Granted, the laboratory, unlike the grapevine, knows no seasons; but in a larger sense this, too, is a springtime phenomenon. For

are we not, as we are told, in the springtime of a new age, the Age of Aquarius? The revolutions of the zodiac may also have their winters and their springs, measured not in months but in centuries. So now, as always, Dionysus shows himself in his traditional forms —alluring, pansexual; madness reigns, an urge to dance comes over people, a trance-inducing beat can be heard from the mountains, and the wine is uncorked.

*B*ut if Dionysus is resisted, either collectively or individually, he comes with superhuman power to rend you apart. And first to go is the head, the seat of the intellect. Not for nothing are today's drug cultists called "heads." They, too, have been seized, in the springtime of a new eon, by the whirlwind of Dionysus's power and, like all victims of the terrible tensions such an invasion brings on, they have lost their heads from their bodies, and Dionysus carries them off in frightful triumph.

A story theatre playwright who formerly taught classics at Yale, Kenneth Cavander has written for HORIZON *on the ancient Near Eastern goddess Astarte. His article about the Russian mystic G. I. Gurdjieff begins on page 58 of this issue.*

Un Massacre du Printemps

Igor Stravinsky's revival of an ancient blood rite produced the primordial happening of the century

On May 29, 1913, at the newly inaugurated Théâtre des Champs Elysées, Sergei Diaghilev presented the première of Igor Stravinsky's *Le Sacre du Printemps* (*The Rite of Spring*) before an audience composed of the most elegant women, the most fashionable young people, the most famous artists, the richest financiers, and the most arrant snobs in Paris. They had come to see a ballet, but what they got was a battle. No sooner did the performance begin than the first skirmishes erupted in the audience. "People laughed, spat, hissed, imitated animal noises," wrote Jean Cocteau, who was, of course, in the thick of it. "They might have eventually tired themselves out, had not the crowd of aesthetes and a few musicians, carried away by their excessive zeal, insulted and even roughly handled the public in the loges. The uproar degenerated into a fight."

Standing in her box, her tiara askew, the dowager Countess de Pourtales flourished her fan and shouted, "It's the first time in sixty years that anyone has dared to make a fool of me!" Maurice Ravel, the best known of the younger French composers, politely requested a fashionable neighbor to be quiet so that he could hear the music, and was called a "dirty Jew" for his pains. But the *beau monde* was divided in its sympathies. One society lady spat in the face of a demonstrator; another, beautifully dressed, slapped the face of a man who was hissing in the next box. Her escort rose, and cards were exchanged; a duel was to be arranged between them.

Two thickset American ladies, Ger-

trude Stein and Alice B. Toklas, were distracted by a man in the next box brandishing his cane: "and finally in a violent altercation with an enthusiast in the box next to him, his cane came down and smashed the opera hat the other had just put on in defiance. It was all incredibly fierce."

For most of the audience, the noise drowned out the music. In the orchestra pit the young conductor, Pierre Monteux, threw desperate glances toward the director's box, but he had orders not to interrupt the performance under any circumstances. The manager of the theatre, Gabriel Astruc, who had put up half a million francs to guarantee *Sacre* and the season, stood in the box shouting, "First listen, then hiss!" Beside him—and beside himself—was Diaghilev, the director of the Ballet Russe, vainly pleading, "*Je vous en prie, laissez achever le spectacle!*" They ordered the house lights turned on in order to quiet the audience, and to let the police pick out and eject the worst troublemakers.

*T*he thirty-year-old composer of the ballet had left the auditorium at the first sign of trouble and had gone backstage to watch the uproar from the wings. "I have never again been that angry," Stravinsky recalled in later years. "The music was so familiar to me; I loved it, and I could not understand why people who had not yet heard it wanted to protest in advance . . . For the rest of the performance I stood in the wings behind Nijinsky holding the tails of his *frac*, while he stood on a chair shouting numbers to

the dancers, like a coxswain." Nijinsky, the ballet's twenty-three-year-old choreographer, was hammering out the rhythm with both his fists and shouting *"Ras, dwa, tri"* to give the dancers their cues.

The ballerina Lydia Sokolova, then a member of the *corps de ballet*, reported afterward: "We were all terrified that we were doing the fourth, fifth or sixth steps, while somebody else was doing the second; and Nijinsky was in the wings stamping and trying to count for different groups all at once. We could see Diaghilev, too, walking up and down, holding his head. We must have been a lovely picture for the audience, racing round, jumping, turning, and wondering when the whole thing was going to collapse."

What they were watching, had they only known it, was the aboriginal Happening of the twentieth century—and the great leap backward to primitive principles which was to lead "classical" music out of its rhythmic decadence and inertia. *Sacre*, as everyone knows by now, is a powerfully kinetic and by no means unmelodious score: it is also a deliberate reversion to the primordial emotions that the ballet had, in fact, instantly aroused in its audience. The very frenzy of their response was an indication of how well the creators of *Sacre* had succeeded in returning the ritual of ballet to its earliest origins. Here was the birth of tragedy from the spirit of paganism as the modern mind envisioned it: herd instinct and tribal rite, nature worship and human sacrifice. The scenario, as summarized by Cocteau, is as follows:

By FREDERIC V. GRUNFELD

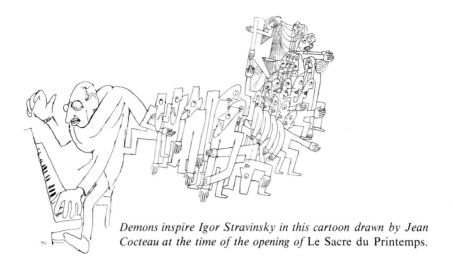

Demons inspire Igor Stravinsky in this cartoon drawn by Jean Cocteau at the time of the opening of Le Sacre du Printemps.

First Tableau. The prehistoric youth of Russia are engaged in springtide games and dances; they worship the earth, and the wise elder reminds them of the sacred rites.

Second Tableau. These simple men believe that the sacrifice of a young girl, chosen from among all her peers, is necessary in order that spring may recommence. She is left alone in the forest; the ancestors come out of the shadows like bears, and form a circle. They inspire the chosen one with the rhythm of a long-drawn-out convulsion. When she falls dead, the ancestors draw near, receive her body and raise it toward heaven.

It was a ballet without the conventional romantic interest, ostensibly close to the dawn of civilization but perhaps closer to the end of it. Stravinsky, for his part, may have been less interested in primitive man than in the musical possibilities of "barbaric" rhythms. Rhythm becomes pre-eminent in *Sacre* and is hammered home by irregular salvos of percussion artillery: 2/8, 3/16, 2/16, 3/16, 2/8, 2/16, 3/16, in adjoining measures and constantly shifting accents. By reaching back to basic musical impulses, Stravinsky created one of the seminal works of the century, like Picasso's African-inspired *Demoiselles d'Avignon*—a score so important as to be considered the birth certificate of contemporary music.

Unlike some of the other ballets he wrote for Diaghilev, *Sacre* had been Stravinsky's own idea from the very first. It occurred to him in St. Petersburg in 1910, as he was working on the last pages of *The Firebird*. "I had a fleeting vision which came to me as a complete surprise, my mind at that moment being full of other things. I saw in imagination a solemn pagan rite: sage elders, seated in a circle, watched a young girl dance herself to death. They were sacrificing her to propitiate the god of spring." The vision impressed both Diaghilev and their mutual friend Nicholas Roerich, a painter who specialized in pagans and primitives. It was Roerich who had designed for Diaghilev a brilliantly executed backdrop for the Polovtsian Dances in *Prince Igor*: a Central Asian landscape dominated by a sulfurous sky that gave French audiences an "indescribable impression of space, emptiness and desolation."

Roerich, still in his thirties, had a passion for Asian folklore that was to turn him into a Tibetan explorer. Alexandre Benois, another Russian painter in Diaghilev's circle, described him as a man utterly absorbed in dreams of prehistoric life—"of the days when the vast limitless plains of Russia and the shores of her lakes and rivers were peopled with the forefathers of the present inhabitants." Benois even suggests that the theme of *Sacre* must have been inspired by the painter; in any case, Roerich agreed to become Stravinsky's collaborator on the ballet, and he appears as co-author on the title page of the score.

At this point in his development Stravinsky, too, subscribed to the cult of neopaganism. He conceived of his work as belonging "to some dark epoch at the beginning of time, to a land without a name, where a people of no nationality celebrated fearful rites to appease an unknown god." But physically he was a most unlikely-looking primitive. At thirty, as the novelist Romain Rolland described him, he was "short, puny-looking, ugly, a yellowish face, thin and tired, a narrow forehead, his hair thin at the top, his eyes behind his pince-nez wrinkled, a fleshy nose and thick lips, the length of his face out of proportion with the size of his forehead." Yet at the same time: "He is very intelligent and simple in his manner; he speaks fluently though he sometimes has to seek French words; and everything he says is original and carefully thought out, whether true or not."

To prepare the scenario of *Sacre*, Stravinsky went to meet Roerich at a country estate near Smolensk that belonged to the Princess Tenichev, one of the great art patrons of Czarist Russia. Since passenger trains ran infrequently, Stravinsky bribed his way onto a freight train and rode to Smolensk in a cattle car containing, besides himself, one unattended bull. "The bull was leashed by a single not-very-reassuring rope, and as he glowered and slavered I began to barricade myself behind my one small suitcase. I must have looked an odd sight at Smolensk as I stepped from that *corrida* carrying my expensive (or, at least, not tramplike) bag and brushing my clothes and hat, but I must also have looked relieved."

*R*oerich showed him a mass of material from the princess's superb collection of Russian folk art and peasant costumes, some of which he adapted as costumes for *Sacre*. His two backdrops again suggested the vast empty spaces of Polovtsian Russia, and the title they agreed on was *Vesna Sviaschennaia*—"Sacred Spring." The French title was suggested later by another member of Diaghilev's inner circle, the painter Léon Bakst.

Stravinsky composed nearly all of the music at a muted piano in a tiny room in the house he rented in Clarens, Switzerland, during the

Nijinsky primps, Stravinsky frets, in this amiable Cocteau cartoon.

following autumn. The score was completed "in a state of exaltation and exhaustion" by the spring of 1912, but Diaghilev waited a year before putting it into production, perhaps because he regarded *Petrouchka* as a necessary intermediate step between *Firebird* and *Sacre*.

Diaghilev, just turned forty, was prepared to stake a great deal on *Sacre*. Brought up in the Urals, far from Moscow or St. Petersburg, he had what Benois called "Scythian" inclinations and was something of a pagan Russian himself. Since his triumphal season of 1908, when he had brought Chaliapin to Paris to sing the title role in *Boris Godunov,* he had given France and western Europe a series of breathtaking initiations into Russian achievements in opera, painting, and above all, the dance. Pavlova and Nijinsky, Fokine and Karsavina, were introduced to Paris under Diaghilev's aegis. Soon his Ballet Russe became something more than a showcase for Russian talent: described by *Le Figaro* as *"ce bazar séduisant de sons et de couleurs exotiques,"* his laboratory served as a focal point of the international avant-garde and as the snob center of Europe.

But Diaghilev never catered to the snobs; he merely exploited them for his own artistic purposes. A big man, with a monocle, whom Cocteau caricatured as a sort of Hindu elephant god of good fortune, he had the manners of a *grand seigneur* and the promotional instincts of a Hollywood mogul. Stravinsky, who was discovered by Diaghilev but later outgrew him, had enormous respect for his energy and integrity as well as his culture and intelligence: "Diaghilev knew how to create around him amazing activity and an artistic

atmosphere that was like an electric current which stimulated all his associates into work, sharpened their fantasy, and made any task seem worth doing. One forgot effort and fatigue. Carried away by this fever of work one became intoxicated with the sense of participation in a creation pure and disinterested."

The one area in which Diaghilev displayed something less than complete disinterestedness was in his relationship with Nijinsky. He had fallen in love with Nijinsky when he was still a fledgling dancer at the Imperial Ballet in St. Petersburg. It was largely on his account that Diaghilev abandoned art exhibitions and opera productions to concentrate on creating a permanent ballet company. But, although Nijinsky became the idol of the Paris ballet world, which preferred him even to Pavlova, he presented something of a problem to Diaghilev because he was not very bright. "In those days he was almost a boy," Benois writes. "Indeed he really remained a boy until the moment when he was overwhelmed by the insanity that cut short his career. He was of uninteresting appearance, rather short of stature, with a thick neck and large head. His features were almost vulgar, of slightly Mongolian type. He seldom opened his mouth to speak, and when he did, blushed violently, would become muddled, then silent . . . Diaghilev used to feel embarrassed for his friend." An astonishing metamorphosis took place the moment he donned his costume and stepped into a role. "At the final rehearsals Nijinsky seemed to awaken from a sort of lethargy; he began to think and feel," Benois observes. "He became reincarnated and actually *entered* into his new existence, as an exceptionally attractive and poetic personality."

The trouble was that Diaghilev insisted on trying to turn Nijinsky into a choreographer. The first ballet assigned

to him, Debussy's *Afternoon of a Faun,* caused a stir with its suggestion of untrammeled sexuality. Then he was entrusted with the two most important ballets for the 1913 season—*Sacre* and Debussy's *Jeux* (Games). Debussy was appalled by the choreography of *Jeux*: "This fellow adds up demi-semi-quavers with his feet, proves the result with his arms, and then, as if suddenly struck with paralysis of one side, listens for a while to the music disapprovingly. This, it appears, is to be called 'stylization of gesture.'"

There was endless trouble over the choreography of *Sacre,* which required 120 rehearsals and then was dropped from the repertoire after six performances. Nijinsky wanted to project the superstitious fear that underlies the ritual of human sacrifice: the movements of the dancers, noted the critic M. D. Calvocoressi, "had been made as constrained, gawky, and heavy as possible, in order to evoke the primitive, apprehensive quality of the men and women of the stone age, struggling against the awesome forces of nature arrayed against them." Nijinsky's choreography fell far short of realizing his intentions: he worked out some of the individual rhythmic patterns provided by the music, but failed to co-ordinate them into a unified whole. Stravinsky, who thought him something of a fool, recalled that what the dancers were doing often had nothing to do with the music.

"Nijinsky," he later wrote, " was incapable of giving intelligible form" to *Sacre*. And indeed, old photographs show some curious things happening: the adolescents, with their toes turned in, heads cocked to one side, looking like premature hippies in their embroidered headbands and peasant blouses,

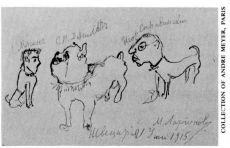

A hostile view: Stravinsky and allies as dogs.

long skirts and sandals. Stravinsky said indignantly that they made his *Danse des adolescents* resemble the gyrations of a group of knock-kneed, long-braided Lolitas.

Whatever the faults or merits of the production, all that has survived of Diaghilev's brilliant *mélange* is the musical component. The music, of course, is now triumphantly "classical" and utterly vindicated. Despite its vicissitudes, it was never in any real danger of being mistaken for anything less than an epoch-making work. That much was apparent even before the première, when Stravinsky tried it out on his friend Debussy, then in his early fifties but already the Grand Old Man of French music. He brought a four-hand piano arrangement of the score: Debussy played the bass part, Stravinsky the treble. "His sight was not improved by his glasses," wrote the critic Louis Laloy, who was present, "and pointing his nose to the keyboard and sometimes humming a part that had been omitted from the arrangement, he led into a welter of sound the supple, agile hands of his friend. Debussy followed without a hitch and seemed to make light of the difficulty. When they finished there was no question of embracing, nor even of compliments. We were dumbfounded, overwhelmed by this hurricane which had come from the depths of the ages and which had taken life by the roots."

Debussy's reaction is particularly significant on two counts: because it seemed at the time that *Sacre* was the very antithesis of the diaphanous sounds the impressionists tried to achieve, and because Stravinsky realized in later years that *Sacre* "owes more to Debussy than to anyone except myself, the best music as well as the worst." Perhaps this is another way of saying that modern music always rebels against what it imitates, and vice versa. *Sacre* was unmistakably anti-Debussian in its rhythmic shock treatments. Yet Debussy said that he admired the savagery of this "primitive music with every modern convenience,"

Cocteau's Nijinsky as a faun.

and declared himself stupefied and haunted as by a "beautiful nightmare." It was only later, in the last depressing years of his life, that he began to pick at flaws.

By that time, *Sacre* had begun leading a life of its own in the concert hall, where it could be judged on strictly musical merits. At the first concert performance, conducted by Monteux at the Casino de Paris in 1914, Stravinsky had the satisfaction of seeing a complete reversal of the original verdict at the ballet, summed up by the press as *Un Massacre du Printemps*. This time the audience rose to its feet and cheered; afterward a crowd swept backstage and hoisted the composer to its shoulders for a triumphal procession through the streets.

*W*hen the guns of August began booming, both admirers and detractors tended to reinterpret *Sacre* as a kind of terrible prophecy. "I see in it the prelude to the war," Cocteau wrote in 1918. And Rolland noted in his diary of the war years: "Stravinsky's assaults of violence and frenetic intoxication, this grotesque hysteria full of fury and absurdity, seems to me to be very much in accord with the great folly of our present epoch, and indeed proclaims it. This frenzy in rhythm is surely the same as that which causes the people of Europe to die and to kill each other."

Since *Sacre* did not arrive in America until 1922, when it was introduced by Stokowski and the Philadelphians, American critics fought a rear-guard action against it long after the Europeans had made their peace with the work. (All except the Soviet musical

establishment, that is: *Sacre* was not heard in Russia for forty years because it supposedly expressed "savagery and bestial instincts" and its composer was "an artistic ideologist of the imperialist bourgeoisie.")

But in both its immediate influence and its long-range effects, *Sacre* proved to be easily the most influential work of the century. Prokofiev's music, beginning with the *Scythian Suite,* is unthinkable without it. So are, to name just a few, Bartók's *Miraculous Mandarin,* Milhaud's *Création du monde,* Honegger's *Pacific 231,* Copland's *Appalachian Spring,* and Varèse's *Ionization.* But the delightful thing about the arts is that the creative imagination is utterly uncomputerlike in its workings, and every new development is fraught with paradoxes. In this case, what was a starting point for everyone else became, for Stravinsky, an ending. While waiting for *Sacre* to be produced he was already plotting *Les Noces,* a work as cerebral and astringent as *Sacre* is full-blooded and sensuous. From there his path led by quick steps to an almost monastic asceticism of sound—to *Apollon Musagètes* and the still more Apollian *Agon.*

In his later years Stravinsky came steadily closer to a taciturn kind of music that lives just next door to silence. Since this was less to the public taste than *Sacre,* he was always being asked to return to his earlier manner—something he stoutly refused to do. He was probably incapable of it. When he lived in California he was approached by a famous violinist who "wanted something that would have the attractiveness of the *best* Stravinsky," and suggested to the composer that the literature of the violin deserved a concerto corresponding to such admirable music as *Le Sacre du Printemps.* To which Stravinsky answered drily that he was "not interested in decadent music." But that may have been rather too harsh a judgment of a work that had transformed the rites of pagan Russia into the Global Village's first dance ritual.

THE KEEPER OF THE GOLDEN BOUGH

It was Sir James Frazer who showed us the rites behind the rites: when we observe Easter or encourage our children's mild-mannered May Day celebrations, we walk in the ghostly footsteps of men who worshiped plants and murdered kings

Sir James Frazer in 1937, aged eighty-three

The scene is idyllic at first: a sunlit Italian landscape just outside Rome; a small lake nestling in a hollow of the Alban hills, and by its shore the grove that is the heart of the mystery. Once it was sacred to the goddess Diana, and its guardian in ancient times lived and died by a strange rule. It is here that the story begins. "In this sacred grove there grew a certain tree round which at any time of the day, and probably far into the night, a grim figure might be seen to prowl. In his hand he carried a drawn sword, and he kept peering warily about him as if at every instant he ex-

pected to be set upon by an enemy. He was a priest and a murderer; and the man for whom he looked was sooner or later to murder him and hold the priesthood in his stead. Such was the rule of the sanctuary."

These words from the opening of Sir James Frazer's *The Golden Bough* begin one of the longest, strangest, and most exotic detective stories in the history of scholarship. Why was the succession to the priesthood of Diana's grove at Nemi decided by mortal combat, and why was the victorious priest, while his precarious term lasted, also given the title of

king? Why did the challenger, a runaway slave, have first to pluck a branch from a certain sacred tree before he could claim the right of combat? And what could such a rite, with its haunting evocation of many other practices sanctioned or required by prescientific ideas in every part of the world, reveal about the intellectual evolution of mankind? These questions set Frazer off on a scholarly quest that was to occupy him for more than a quarter of a century, and whose results, expanding from a mere two volumes in 1890 to an eventual thirteen in the years between 1907

By JOHN W. BURROW

and 1915, were to make him probably the most famous anthropologist of all time.

The solemn richness of Frazer's language, the drama and hushed suspense with which he invests the sinister scene by the peaceful wooded lake, and the feeling for the mystery and poetry inherent in uncovering the dark roots of primitive savagery and superstition are typical of the qualities that gave *The Golden Bough* an influence with the general educated public such as no other anthropological work has ever had. Readers were dazzled, too, by the sheer scope and erudition of a book that linked the ancient Greeks to the modern Eskimos and the rituals of Central African tribes to the seasonal festivals of English rustics. It was a book that truly seemed to take the whole world and human history for its subject, making it what Frazer himself called "an epic of humanity."

Everywhere, essentially, the human mind obeyed the same laws; everywhere reason and science were preceded by superstition in its successive forms of magic and religion, often manifested in bizarre, ludicrous, or appalling ways,

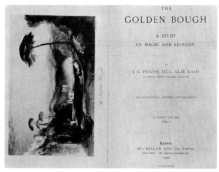

One masterpiece begets another: Sir James gleaned title, inspiration, and frontispiece for The Golden Bough *from a J. M. W. Turner painting, top—a romantic's vision of ancient rites at Diana's Lake Nemi sanctuary.*

19

but always, if approached in the right manner—that is, scientifically and comparatively—ultimately intelligible. The apparently endless litany of names, examples, and comparisons was intoned by a master of vivid, opulent prose, which touched its weird subject matter with irony and pathos and a kind of magisterial, classical serenity.

It is appropriate to introduce Frazer by his greatest work, for *The Golden Bough* grew in bulk, reputation, and influence until it must have seemed utterly to dwarf the tiny, tongue-tied Scotsman, with the shining blue eyes and pointed beard, whose molelike toil had created it. Sir James Frazer, as he became in 1914, was exceptionally industrious and exceptionally henpecked. These two qualities were to become almost legendary.

James George Frazer was born in 1854, and one feels that it is typical of the somewhat obsessive regularity of his habits that the date should have been January 1. His parents, both of Glasgow merchant stock, were deeply religious, and strict observance of the Sabbath and daily reading of the Bible were part of the family way of life. Frazer's boyhood seems to have been a happy one, and in later life he wrote with deep affection of his home at Helensburgh, "the little white town by the sea," on the estuary of the Clyde. Even after Frazer turned away from the Christian certainties of his parents' creed, there seems to have been no family breach, and his mother died with her hand resting on one of her famous son's books. On Frazer, the family Bible reading left its mark. Belief disappeared but veneration of a sort remained, and one of his works was a selection of passages from the Bible "chosen for their literary beauty and interest."

At Glasgow University he encountered certainties of another kind, and these never left him: classical learning and physical science, nature's laws and the regimental precision of Latin syntax. Frazer never learned to carry his youthful learning lightly. There is a story that later on, when he was an internationally famous scholar, Frazer learned of a small grammatical error in a Latin sentence he had published and immediately offered his resignation to the head of his college. He refused to accept Einstein's theory of relativity because it conflicted with the teaching of the great nineteenth-century physicist Lord Kelvin, whose lectures he had attended as an undergraduate. Freud, whose own *Totem and Taboo* was another of the books heavily indebted to Frazer's work, he also rejected, perhaps partly from prudishness. Frazer was, after all, a Victorian, and his accounts of the fertility cults to which he devoted so much attention sometimes remind one forcibly of what might be called the "nameless abominations" school of nineteenth-century ethnographic description.

Frazer was rooted in the century of his birth, and his mind lost its elasticity fairly early. It is characteristic that when, in old age, he became blind, the books his secretaries had to read endlessly for his amusement were his own works, to which he would listen "as if hearing for the first time the words of a promising colleague."

*V*irtually all Frazer's adult life was spent in Cambridge as a fellow of Trinity College, where he occupied rooms beside the great gate, on a staircase that in the past had housed Isaac Newton, the historian Macaulay, and William Makepeace Thackeray. Frazer wrote one of his word pictures of the scene: "the tranquil court of an ancient college, where the sundial marks the silent passage of the hours, and in the long summer days the fountain plashes drowsily amid flowers and grass; where, as the evening shadows deepen, the lights come out in the blazoned windows of the Elizabethan hall, and from the chapel the sweet voices of the choir, blent with the pealing music of the organ, float on the peaceful air, telling of man's eternal aspirations after truth and goodness and immortality." Frazer's books—all twenty thousand of them—eventually became too heavy for the ceiling of the room below, and he had to move across the road, to a part of the college that even his eloquence could hardly have made anything but dank, gloomy, and squalid.

Frazer began his scholarly career as a classicist and humanist, a student of ancient civilization, and never altogether ceased to be one. Anthropologists were sometimes puzzled as to whether they were dealing with one of themselves or with a classical scholar who had trespassed with outstanding success upon their discipline. Frazer himself spoke of *The Golden Bough* sometimes as science, sometimes as literature. Certainly he was always an intensely self-conscious stylist, a topographic and dramatic scene-painter, an artist in words. In many pages of Frazer's anthropological writings one can recognize the classical scholar who had tramped around Greece for his edition of the works of the ancient Greek traveler Pausanias and who had supplied from his own observation, in the lush prose of his footnotes, the color and particularity of scene that Pausanias had unfortunately failed to provide. To Frazer places were never, if he could help it, bald geographic designations; they came in a package complete with vegetation and meteorology: "the blue skies of Arizona or the rain-saturated forests of British Columbia."

It is ironic, however, that the only fieldwork Frazer ever did was while editing a classical Greek text. For Frazer's life was unadventurous even by the standards of nineteenth-century anthropology. He was tongue-tied and self-effacing; he hated and avoided controversy and suffered badly from stage fright when he had to lecture. He took no part in university politics or administration, and when he accepted the chair of anthropology at Liverpool University, he quickly discovered his mistake and resigned after a year. Even to try to imagine the mannered classicist Frazer, who found all human contacts painfully difficult, as a possible field anthropologist in a primitive society, seems almost an act of cruelty. When the philosopher William James once asked him if he had ever met a savage, his reply was "Heaven forbid."

This repudiation was to him, however, not so much a rejection of danger and discomfort as an assertion of scientific objectivity. Frazer always stressed the danger to the comparative anthropologist of too much immersion in one particular area. The anthropologist was to be a kind of clearinghouse, receiving, organizing, and putting into perspective the precious data about the primitive peoples of the world before it was too late, before native ways of life were adulterated or obliterated by the encroachments of Western civilization. The collectors of this information were to be missionaries, traders, explorers, and administrators, whose daily lives brought them into contact with primitive societies. Frazer's initiative lay only in maintaining a vast correspondence with them and drawing up a table of questions for their use. But they were to be eyes and ears only, and to keep as free as possible from theorizing, which might prejudice their vision. One of Frazer's chief informants was explicitly forbidden to read books so that he might keep his powers of observation untainted.

At the center of the web sat Frazer, the mastermind, in his quiet Cambridge room with the fountain plashing lazily outside the window, collating the odd, extraordinary, sometimes almost unbelievable facts they sent back, tinting their bare reports with artful adjectives and weaving them into a tapestry that he did not know whether to call science or literature. The division of labor that he justified as a requirement of scientific objectivity was, in fact, only another form of the old distinction between the practical man, the man of things, and the scholar, whom Frazer now sometimes called a scientist, the man of words and books. In that sense, Frazer remained the humanist classical scholar, who had won his fellowship with a dissertation on Plato's philosophy, to the end of his days.

But classical scholarship itself, the marble heart of a gentleman's education, was changing in the late nineteenth century under the impact of the new science of anthropology, and Frazer put himself boldly at the head of that change, doing, in his own way, as much as any man to make anthropology academically respectable and to make some knowledge of primitive ways of thought and behavior part of the common cultural experience of Western man. He was able to do it partly because he had a gift for turning uncouth raw materials into a work of art and a vision of a strange world, alien and yet somehow close and almost familiar, which tugged at the imagination and provided poets and literary men with fresh and vital images, in a world where technology and urban civilization seemed to offer nothing but imaginative impoverishment and aridity. But it also mattered that Frazer, as an accomplished classicist and fellow of an ancient college, was at the center of the old gentlemanly culture that had often looked down on anthropology as a collection of nasty trivia.

Classical scholars of Frazer's generation, however, were beginning to think strange thoughts and to see the elegant mythology, the sublime Athenian tragedies, and even the sophisticated philosophical systems of classical antiquity in a new and startling perspective. Behind the Greek drama and festivals like the Olympian games there seemed to lurk other, more bloody and primitive rituals, performed by actors to whom their performance was a matter of life or death.

Classical deities and heroes, Adonis, Hera, Persephone, Dionysus, whose ideal forms so many painters since the Renaissance had depicted, bore traces of cousinship not only, as had long been recognized, with the gods of other elaborate pantheons, Sanskrit, Babylonian, Egyptian, and Norse, but with the images of grass and wood, feathers and sun-baked mud, that were feared and revered by modern savages. Over Diana's chilly classical shoulder, like an uncouth relative insisting on an embarrassing kinship, leered a fat-bellied fertility goddess with pendulous breasts and interestingly unclassical proportions. The dark gods were claiming their place on Olympus.

There was, after all, nothing very surprising about it. According to the prevailing doctrines of social evolution, whose antecedents went back several centuries, all the elements of higher civilizations had sprung from savage roots and bore traces of their origin for those with eyes to see. If man, as Darwin had shown, was cousin to the apes, why should Zeus not submit to being cousin to a juju—different stages of the same mental process? It only remained to amass the evidence and mark the various stages. *The Golden Bough,* ostensibly an inquiry into a particular classical rite and legend, was actually an immense comparative study of primitive magic and superstitution, culminating in a slightly oblique but unmistakable glance at Christianity.

Why, Frazer's argument begins, was the priest of the sacred grove of Nemi also a king? To answer this question, he plunges into what he takes to be the mental world of primitive magical ritual, with its guiding principles of sympathetic magic and taboo. Ignorant of the true relations of cause and effect, "the untutored savage" lives in a world in which any resemblance is enough to establish a relationship or even identity of one class of things with another. Men, beasts, vegetation, and weather are bound promiscuously together in a magical economy in ways for which science and reason offer no warrant, and the means of controlling nature is by ritual imitation of the desired events.

But nature thus treated does not always respond, and magic does not always work; so the momentous transition is made from magic to religion. Natural phenomena are thought of now as capricious deities, who must be made to work for their worshipers. But the heritage of sympathetic magic is not forgotten. The nature gods are personified in priests or divine kings who in a sense *are* the gods and natural forces they represent. The grove at Nemi was sacred to Diana, a goddess of fertility, and her priest was her divine consort, god of the wood and the rain.

Frazer produces an immense number of alleged parallels, from other ancient mythologies, from the phallic gods and fertility goddesses of anthropology and the May kings and queens of European folklore. The function of the divine pair was to ensure continued fertility, and as Frazer rather primly puts it, speaking of the rites performed, "we may assume with a high degree of probability that the profligacy which notoriously attended these ceremonies was at one time not an accidental excess but an essential part of the rites, and that in the opinion of those who performed them the marriage of trees and plants could not be fertile without the real union of the human sexes." For "profligacy," in other words, read sexual intercourse performed as sympathetic magic by nature divinities in human form.

But why, Frazer continues, was the divine king of the grove always killed by his successor? This leads Frazer to the myths of the sacrifice and resurrection of a god, a ritual enactment of the natural miracle performed by the spring of every year. The god is killed in order that he may be renewed, and by his renewal guarantee that of the earth whose powers he embodies. So it was with the Greek Adonis, the Phrygian Attis, the Egyptian Osiris, and the Norse Balder the Beautiful, and so also, Frazer hints, with the founder of Christianity.

There is one last question: why did the challenger for the priesthood of Nemi have first to pluck a branch from a sacred tree, and why was this associated in classical tradition with the golden bough carried by Virgil's hero Aeneas to preserve him on his journey through the kingdom of the dead? Why *golden*? The answer Frazer finds in the myth of Balder. Balder, god of the oak, could be killed only by a piece of mistletoe. Frazer finds mistletoe regarded in the primitive world as the life or external soul of the tree to which it clings. Furthermore, Balder's body, to perform its work of renewal, had first to be consumed by fire; the legend of the phoenix is a variant of the same idea. Fire symbolized the rays of the reviving sun. The color and legendary significance of mistletoe, the golden light of fire and the sun, linked for Frazer the golden bough of Nemi with the fire festivals performed by the peasantry all over Europe at times of solstice and equinox. All elements of fertility and renewal fell into their places in the rite of the sacred grove; the riddle's solution was complete.

*A*t one level, Frazer probably did not greatly care about the riddle. At times he seems almost to tease the reader with the pretense that all this erudition is deployed to provide a dubious interpretation of an obscure rite. For long periods he seems to forget about it altogether. His argument is often stretched to the breaking point by conjecture and remote analogy. "We may suppose that," "it is not impossible that," become more and more frequent introductions to a new line of argument. But far more important than the interpretation of the particular rite is the evolutionary drama of the transition from magic to religion and the theories of the mental processes underlying them. Frazer's interest was in primitive psychology. Even here he frequently changed his interpretations, professing to present them as purely provisional; it was, he would sometimes say, the facts that mattered, not the theories built on them.

Modern anthropologists have objected not merely to Frazer's particular interpretations, such as that magic always precedes religion or that primitives have no notion of cause and effect (when all the evidence indicates that they do), but to his whole strategy, to the way his examples are presented

1. SACRED MARRIAGE

The scene of intimate contact between Seti I and the fertility goddess Isis on a temple relief, above, assured ancient Egyptians that 1300 B.C. would be a prosperous year. Egyptians believed that their welfare depended on the Pharaoh's magical ability to coax favors for his people from the gods. If Seti could win caresses from Isis, he could also secure from her the promise of a plentiful harvest. Frazer observed that priest-kings of many primitive planting cultures ensured the earth's fertility through sacred intercourse with the goddess of vegetation—or her human representative. Modern-day May kings and queens are the innocent vestiges of these early orgiastic unions.

5. THE CORN SPIRIT

A slight sprinkling of holy water ensures the health and vigor of the vegetation spirit embodied by this straw-clad European harvest celebrant. But ancient peoples used more violent measures to preserve the vitality of the force that animated their crops. According to Frazer, most primitive people believed that the slowest and laziest worker, the one who harvested the last sheaf of corn, acquired the spirit that lurked there. To prevent the corn spirit from absorbing its captor's weakness, the people killed and devoured the last harvester. The corn spirit passed to a younger, more zestful man.

2. TABOOS ON THE PRIEST-KING

The high priest was both god and slave to the Central American Zapotecs who fashioned this imposing clay image of their pontiff about A.D. 1050. Only the priest had the power to win favors from the gods for his people. When he passed by, his subjects fell to the earth in awe. But he was forbidden to look at the sun, or to touch the ground, or to have intercourse with women. The slightest irregularity in conduct might impair the priest's powers, and bring an end to prosperity. Frazer noted that many primitive societies zealously enslaved their priest-kings with rigid taboos to preserve his strength. Two centuries ago the Japanese emperor was forbidden to cut his fingernails, lest this disrupt the customary order of the universe.

3. KILLING THE KING

Our tranquil Easter observances probably grew out of bloody heathen rituals. Francesco del Cossa's fifteenth-century portrayal of the Crucifixion echoes the ancient anguish of dying kings. Frazer detected a pattern of systematic regicide in many primitive societies. Since an enfeebled king was useless to cultures dependent on his potency in magic ritual, aspirants regularly challenged him to tests of strength. If the king lost, he was slaughtered and his powers were resurrected in the victor. Frazer suggests that the early church, anxious to win converts, chose to observe Christ's Passion on the date of king-slaying in other cultures. Pantomime regicide persists today: in parts of Bavaria vigorous youths pretend to murder the Whitsuntide king.

4. THE DYING AND REVIVING GODS

Total devastation threatened Greece before the mythological event represented on this fifth-century B.C. vase. Tormented by her daughter Persephone's abduction to the underworld, the vegetation goddess Demeter, right, ravaged the land with famine. Then Persephone rose from her subterranean prison, left, and her mother blessed Greece with the gift of agriculture. Each winter Persephone had to visit her underworld captor, but her return in the spring brought life to the winter fields. Frazer saw that most primitive planting societies acted out the sacred drama of a dying and reviving god to ensure new vegetation in the spring. As late as this century, Russian peasants staged the death and resurrection of the vegetation spirit Kostrubunko.

6. EXPULSION OF EVILS

The sorrows of the nation die with the burning image of the demon spirit Ravana in a modern Hindu ceremony derived from ancient purification rituals. Frazer found that primitive men thought swarming multitudes of malevolent spirits caused the diseases, losses, and mishaps that tormented them and diminished their crops. Periodically, many early cultures staged a desperate hunt to expel these devils. Magical skills enabled them to transfer the evil spirits to a community scapegoat, often the dying god of vegetation. When they destroyed the god, his image, or his human representative, they purged the land of its accumulated troubles and sins.

7. PERIODS OF LICENSE

The explosive burst of merrymaking at a modern Brazilian carnival, above, echoes the ecstasies of ancient agricultural rites. Frazer found that at planting time, many primitive people indulged in activities and emotional excesses that were forbidden during other seasons of the year. In a mock ceremony a slave or felon assumed the role of king and presided while the mightiest and the lowliest members of the community mingled in endless displays of gluttony, intoxication, frenzied dancing, and sexual abandon. By releasing their own imprisoned passions, the people hoped to provoke the seeds they had sown to a similar outpouring of latent energy.

8. FIRE FESTIVALS

Bodies as well as souls are uplifted by the prolonged sunshine of a Midsummer Day in Bavaria. As the year's longest day slides into night, Bavarians compete in traditional bonfire-leaping contests, above. Amid this merriment, few wonder why the day brings such customs. But Frazer was curious. He traced bonfire festivals to ancient rites designed to keep the sun at its midsummer zenith. The human representative of the vegetation deity was fuel for early bonfires. By feeding the god to the fire, the people guaranteed the persistence of sun for their crops and the extinction of evil influences. The tallest crops came to the couple leaping highest over the flames.

torn from their social context of habitual everyday behavior and strung together to form a speculative evolutionary sequence of primitive metaphysical ideas. Examples presented in this way were considerably more entertaining than the tables of kinship relations and the like that make such an effective deterrent to reading modern anthropology, but they are also seriously misleading. It is as though one were to portray the American mentality entirely from behavior at Thanksgiving, July 4, Christmas, and New Year's Eve. A foreign people presented in this way, as every travel agent knows, is apt to sound more amiable, more childlike, and a good deal sillier than it is.

This, however, was the common anthropological practice of Frazer's time, and his early readers could feel that they were being given the latest results of anthropological science in exceptionally palatable form. Frazer's book is a product of four centuries of European superiority and domination, a map of the soul of the undeveloped world and of Europe's own savage past fossilized in the customs and superstitions of her peasantry. It was a kind of Victorian or Edwardian lantern lecture, on a vast scale and in gorgeous colors, with the voice of the lecturer, calm and ironic, coming reassuringly out of the darkness.

Did one want to know of the absurd behavior of the Wawamba, the quaint superstitions of Breton peasants, the magical lore of the ancient Greeks, or the atrocious practices of the Dieri? Frazer could tell one. Readers could smile over stories of tribes who worshiped Queen Victoria or tried to copulate with trees. There were, it appeared, men on earth who would die if they spoke to their mothers-in-law; there were sorcerers who kept asylums for stray souls, and if you had lost yours, would supply you with a new one for a fixed fee. Savages, with Frazer as their impresario, provided an endlessly fascinating menagerie of exotic human behavior.

It was all splendid stuff for the cynical 1920's, when Frazer's reputation was at its height, just as the superior tone and faith in science and the pomp and circumstance of Frazer's prose appealed to the age of confidence and imperial grandeur that was passing away. Frazer's very inconsistencies and hesitations made his work acceptable to men of a wide variety of creeds and temperaments. The savage was absurd and one could look down on him, but he was also uncomfortably close, as well as rich food for the imagination. Science was destined everywhere to supersede and extinguish superstition—but was it? Frazer, like his contemporary Freud, another rationalist who devoted his life to studying the irrational, had a powerful and alarmed sense that underneath the civilized and rational surface of life there lay a dormant volcano of nonrational forces.

*B*eneath the confident evolutionist in Frazer there was a Manichaean who alternated between optimism and gloom. More persistent than any particular theory in his work, as Stanley Edgar Hyman has pointed out, were certain pervasive metaphors, especially light and the sun, and its opposite, darkness and gloom, so suitable to represent primeval forests and the confused thoughts of ignorant and frightened men. It is this as much as anything that gives *The Golden Bough* its literary zest; its pages abound in "gloomy recesses," "dark labyrinths," "phantasmagoria," and "subterranean forces." One is caught up in the drama of a dark and sleeping earth warmed into renewed life by the reviving sun, which also seems in the end to symbolize, for author and reader, the illumination of a dark world by knowledge and science.

Not the least of *The Golden Bough's* excitements for its readers were its references to a ritual and pagan origin of the central mysteries of Christianity. Eating the god—the title of one of Frazer's chapters—was a common ritual practice, rooted in magic. So was hanging divine scapegoats on a tree and even piercing their sides with a spear, that they might take upon themselves the sins of the people. The dying fall with which Frazer's immense book ends is obviously modeled on Gibbon's account of the moment that inspired the theme of his *Decline and Fall of the Roman Empire*: the sound of the barefooted Christian friars chanting in the Roman temple of Jupiter—"the triumph of barbarism and of religion." Frazer writes instead of a twilight of the gods, in a supremely effective elegiac passage, almost every word of which has been charged with meaning by what has gone before.

The great winding journey over, we return at last to Nemi. It is evening and and "we look back and see the sky aflame with sunset, its golden glory resting like the aureole of a dying saint over Rome and touching with a crest of fire the dome of St. Peter's. The sight once seen can never be forgotten." The King of the Wood has gone, "But Nemi's woods are still green, and as the sunset fades above them in the west, there comes to us, borne on the swell of the wind, the sound of the church bells of Aricia ringing the Angelus. *Ave Maria! . . . Le roi est mort, vive le roi! Ave Maria!*"

Frazer was not the first to be inspired by the image of the golden bough and its legendary association with the groves of Nemi. Apart from Virgil, the painter Turner had depicted the scene in a painting that Frazer used as the original frontispiece to *The Golden Bough*. Macaulay had written a verse:

The still glassy lake that sleeps
Beneath Aricia's trees—
Those trees in whose dim shadow
The ghastly priest doth reign
The priest who slew the slayer,
And shall himself be slain.

But whatever the eventual verdict on Frazer's book as a work of anthropological science, one thing is certain. Frazer has taken possession of the grove of Nemi and its associated legend more tenaciously than any of its desperate priestly kings, and it belongs now, not to the Latin poet, the English painter, or the great historian, but to

The Sunday Times, TOPIX, LONDON

James Frazer. He, if anyone, is the King of the Wood.

The vast bulk and learning of *The Golden Bough* and the long list of Frazer's other works were the product of an astounding industry. There is something almost stupefying about the accounts of the sheer mechanical regularity of Frazer's working life, as though he were some half-naked drudge in a mine or factory of the early industrial revolution, instead of a distinguished scholar of worldwide reputation and fellow of a rich and ancient college. The story of Frazer's life is a story of unremitting labor. Day after day, year after year, the same working hours: 4–8 A.M., then breakfast; 9–12, then lunch and a nap; 3–6, then dinner; and finally, work from 7 to midnight.

Bertrand Russell, another fellow of Trinity, mentions only one memory of Frazer. Fellows have free dinners in College Hall, and "as a Scot, Frazer could not ignore this consideration." He grudged, however, "every minute taken from his studies for the gross work of self-nourishment." But fellows who arrived more than a quarter of an hour late were fined. Frazer therefore always arrived exactly a quarter of an hour late.

In 1896 he married a Frenchwoman, Lilly Grove, a widow with two children, but it made no difference. They made a compact that his working hours should remain unchanged, and Frazer worked on his honeymoon. He never broke down and never revolted against this self-imposed slavery; the most he allowed himself was a sort of resigned self-pitying wistfulness in a verse he once wrote:

Still, still I con old pages
And through great volumes wade,
While life's brief summer passes
And youth's brief roses fade.

From the moment of his marriage Frazer entered a new slavery, one accepted with the same unprotesting

The indomitable Lady Frazer, photographed with Sir James on his eighty-third birthday, pressed universities to acclaim the works she forced from her modest, weary, and already famous husband.

meekness. From that point all accounts of Frazer turn out, in fact, to be accounts of Lady Frazer, of her masterfulness, her ambition for her husband, her temper and her meanness, and of how she would make lists of the governments, universities, and learned societies that had not yet given honors to her modest and already much decorated husband and scheme how to induce them to do their duty. When Frazer was aging, tired, and creatively spent, she made him rehash his earlier works until his publisher rebelled; there is perhaps an irony in Frazer's dedication of one book of snippets to her as its "only begetter." "James, go back to your work at once," she was once heard to shout.

Frazer's colleague and admirer the great anthropologist Bronislaw Malinowski described her guardedly as "unquestionably a puzzling element to most of Frazer's friends." A female colleague, uninhibited by chivalry, proposed the passing of "Game Laws for the Preserving of Eminent Husbands." Two of Frazer's secretaries, reading to the old man, over and over, his own works, were struck by his liking for the story of the Witch of Endor and connected his preference with the jealous, grasping, devoted old woman, with the strong French accent, hooked nose, beard, and untidy hair, who still dominated his life.

Few of us are likely to be edifying in our eighties, and the Frazers were harshly afflicted; he became blind and paralyzed, she stone-deaf. Their last years together were pathetic and dreadful, like some pitiless black comedy by August Strindberg. Seated side by side on seats like thrones, her hand possessively on his, they reminded observers of two images from the British Museum. She was as ruthless and strong-willed as ever, her suspiciousness aggravated to frenzy by deafness. All communication with him had to be through her. Frazer was polite, gentle, and fussed obsessively about his secretaries' comfort—was he or she too warm, too much in the light, and so on. Lady Frazer, seeing lips moving, would jealously demand the reason. A note would be written: "HE ASKED IF I WAS TOO WARM." Frazer, unable to see but aware of trouble, would anxiously ask what was the matter, and the tragi-farcical cycle would begin again.

One of Lady Frazer's last victories was to get Trinity College to send Frazer's dinner to their flat, a distance of more than a mile. The meal, covered with a green baize cloth and accompanied by a college servant, would travel through the Cambridge streets to the old man who did not want it, to be pushed into his protesting mouth by the indomitable woman whose will kept him alive and in doing so sustained her own life also.

In 1941, at the age of eighty-seven, Frazer rebelled and, as the saying is, went to his last rest. In less than twenty-four hours, "James, go back to your work at once," echoed in a heavy French accent through eternity. Lady Frazer had caught up with him.

John W. Burrow has written articles for HORIZON *on the lives and ideas of several nineteenth-century philosophers, including Marx, Darwin, and Bentham.*

l'assiette au beurre
1er mai
8 HEURES DE TRAVAIL
8 HEURES DE SOMMEIL
8 HEURES DE LOISIR
grandjouan

THE RITES OF SPRING

MAY DAY

Workers of the world unite! You have nothing to lose but your daisy chains

"Where are the May Days of yesteryear,
When every bourgeois shook with fear
At the sight of our blood-red flag unfurled
O'er the marching hosts of tomorrow's world?"

The poet, a French syndicalist writing in the left-wing teachers' magazine *L'Ecole Emancipée* on May 1, 1928, was exaggerating, but less than poets usually do. A generation earlier the approach of May 1 had regularly filled a part of the European bourgeoisie, and many conservative Americans, with dread. To them, and to some revolutionaries as well, May Day was more than a symbol; it was a dress rehearsal for world revolution.

Naturally, what was a day of dread for the privileged classes had a quite different meaning for the oppressed and exploited masses. For them it was a day not merely for hoping but for forcing hope. It was a day for demanding instead of humbly asking; a day of just and brotherly wrath; a day of risk and sacrifice and struggle. In certain countries—France, for example—striking on May 1 was likely to cost the striker his job, and singing the *Internationale* as he marched behind a red flag was even likelier to cost him a cracked head. Thus, May Day was above all the worker's celebration of his recovered manhood: a day for

WORKMATES OF THE MONTH: *The May Day cover of a French radical journal of 1906 invokes the impossible dream—eight hours each of work, of play, and of sleep per day.*

throwing back his shoulders and looking his own fear—of the police, of his bosses, of hunger—in the eye.

Today, both the heroic and the apocalyptic aspects of May Day have disappeared throughout most of the world. (If there is still an occasional hint of the apocalypse in the date, it is provided by the Red Army's annual unveiling of new weapons at the May 1 ceremonies in Moscow.) The parades or similar demonstrations organized by Communists and other orthodox leftists in many Western cities are at most colorful pageants of class warfare, and no longer its grim reality. The ritual scuffles between police and long-haired young ultraleftists that often break out under the censorious, middle-aged eyes of the party or union bosses are a simple mimicry of revolution. In several capitalist countries May Day has even lost its proletarian character: it is a legal, paid holiday, enjoyed by every class.

Though the gradual transformation of May Day no doubt implies a certain blurring of class antagonisms, to conclude that it marks an irreversible fading of revolutionary tensions, or to regard it as a victory of reason and goodwill over organized hate and greed, would be risky. The phenomenon does, however, reflect the victory of what an old-fashioned historian might call human nature over ideology. More specifically, it demonstrates the built-in resistance of man's collective unconscious to cultural innovation, and

shows how the old gods, when they are overthrown, generally return with new identities to infiltrate and subvert the pantheon of the victors.

The transformation of May 1 from a day of revolutionary dedication into an innocuous public holiday is in large part simply the return of May Day as a traditional Indo-European festival of spring whose basic character seems to have changed astonishingly little in the past few thousand years. Even at its most revolutionary, there was more of the traditional and the bucolic in its rites than its celebrants ever realized.

At the conscious level, it is true, folklore played no part in establishing the modern, revolutionary May Day. The idea of promoting national campaigns for an eight-hour working day by concerted international action on a fixed date seems to have originated in France. At first it was thought of as a one-time affair. The date was agreed on at a congress of socialists from twenty-one countries held in Paris in 1889. As far as is known, the choice was inspired by a message from Samuel Gompers, president of the recently formed American Federation of Labor, announcing that a nationwide program of strikes, parades, and other demonstrations by American workers in support of the eight-hour day had been scheduled for May 1, 1890.

The AFL seems to have hit on May 1 chiefly for practical reasons—in a number of states it was the customary starting day for leases and contracts—

By EDMOND TAYLOR

but a history of struggle, heroism, and tragedy already underscored the date. A similar day of national agitation on May 1, 1886, had won important victories in the fight for shorter working hours. But in Chicago it had also helped detonate an explosion of mob violence—police mob versus worker mob—that culminated in the Haymarket riot on May 4: six policemen killed outright by a bomb, allegedly thrown by an anarchist; a number of men and women shot down by police fire; four necks later broken by the hangman's noose. The worldwide horror and indignation aroused by the affair further influenced the Paris congress to pattern the proposed international program of agitation upon that of the AFL.

*T*he congress's decision passed unnoticed at the time. In France, where it was to be three more years before parliament would get around to fixing a maximum ten-hour working day for children under sixteen, and seventeen years before it decreed a weekly day of rest for all workers, an international campaign for the eight-hour day perhaps sounded so utopian that it was scarcely alarming. The response by workers throughout the industrialized West, however, exceeded expectations. The myth of working-class internationalism began to look less mythical. The success of the May 1 manifestation in 1890 naturally led to its renewal in 1891. This time the European bourgeoisie was worried, if not yet seriously frightened.

There had been almost no violence in 1890, but May 1, 1891, unleashed some real revolutionary passion and simultaneously stimulated the repressive zeal of the police. Savage riots broke out in Rome and Florence. In Hungary furious strikers derailed trains. In the suburbs of Paris workers marching behind a red flag clashed with the police and a bloody gun fight ensued. At Fourmies, in the industrial north of France, there was no gun fight, merely a massacre: soldiers firing into an excited but nonviolent crowd of demonstrators killed ten persons, including a young girl and an eleven-year-old boy.

Indignation over the Fourmies massacre contributed to the militant temper of the socialist congress held in Brussels three months later. At the instigation of the hard-line faction in the Marxist International, the congress voted to make May 1 a permanent institution, as an "affirmation of the class struggle." Thus May Day acquired its specific Marxist-revolutionary character, deplored by the anarchists on the one hand and by the moderate socialists and trade-unionists on the other.

To the hard-liners of the period, May 1 was much more than an annual demonstration of proletarian solidarity and revolutionary spirit. It was a kind of magic weapon against the bourgeois establishment. In France insurrectionary Marxists like Jules Guesde believed that May 1 was "the dynamite which will blow up capitalist society."

Energized by the Russian Revolution of 1905, the huge and vehement May Day demonstrations that year and the next led a number of European bourgeois to suspect that Guesde might be right. In Paris the approach of May 1, 1906, witnessed a flight of capitalists—and capital—from the impending revolutionary terror. Trains were packed; refugees from France filled the hotels in Geneva. Though guarded by some fifty thousand policemen and troops, the bourgeois who remained in Paris, according to the French social historian Maurice Dommanget, stocked their apartments with food as if for a siege. One wealthy Parisian, Dommanget says, brought home a live cow and calf, doubtless to make sure that his *bifteck* and veal roast should not fail, though the heavens fall.

May 1, 1906, was by no means the last May Day fright for the bourgeoisie. May 1, 1919, with the triumphant Bolsheviks setting the tone in Moscow's Red Square and millions of freshly demobilized veterans adrift in the cities of the West, loomed up as even more apocalyptic. Once again, the exaggerated fears of the capitalist elite, interacting with the irrational hopes and well-founded resentments of the revolutionary masses, exploded into widespread violence. The discovery, just before May Day, of bombs addressed to prominent American radical foes set off a nationwide Red Scare. In New York "country boys gaping at the orators in Madison Square," as F. Scott Fitzgerald put it, were brutally ridden down by the police. Police clubs likewise flailed wildly in Cleveland and Boston, and two people were killed. In Paris, plastered with tricolor posters announcing *La Patrie est en Danger*, more than fifty thousand police and soldiers battled with the largest, most aggressive workers' demonstration the city had witnessed since the Commune of 1871. By nightfall two workers lay dead, and there were 428 injured among the law forces alone.

The Great Depression, the civil war between Nazis and Communists before Hitler took power in Germany, and the Popular Front of the 1930's brought violent new May Day clashes in one country or another, but the long-term trend has, so far, been in the opposite direction. Indeed, May 1, 1906, probably marked the apogee of the Guesdeist mystique. A year later, the German socialist Rosa Luxembourg was already lamenting that "the bourgeoisie no longer believes . . . that the very idea of May 1 is already the beginning of the end for capitalism." May Day—except where police overreaction created an atmosphere of violence—was changing. Under its revolutionary trappings, it was turning into the good-natured working-class festival the moderates in the socialist movement had yearned for, and the extremists had bitterly opposed, since the time of the Paris congress of 1889.

*W*hat the theorists of May Day revolution had failed to take into account were the traditional and only partly conscious associations of the date itself. For centuries it had been a particularly relaxed popular holiday, given over to joyous singing, dancing, and courting: lads and lasses making love, not class war, behind every flowering hedge. The ancient Romans, no doubt trying to rationalize more primitive rites of vegetation and fertility magic, telescoped between April 28 and May 3 the festivals of Flora, goddess of flowers, Maia, goddess of growth, and the *lares,* spirits of hearth and field. The first recorded May Day parades were probably made up of flower-decked Romans carrying the enthroned effigy of Maia through the streets. Prostitutes contributed to the vernal spirit by disrobing and posing in alluring attitudes. In honor of the *lares,* slaves, the chief tillers of the soil, were allowed a day of rest, given extra food and wine, and even waited on by their masters, as they were during the December Saturnalia.

The triumph of Christianity and the establishment of the church's own spring rites in the feasts of Good Friday, Easter, and Pentecost failed to alter radically the observance of May 1 as an unofficial holiday. The rationalizing myths vanished, but the magic ceremonies associated with the day survived down to the industrial age. So did the attendant mood of joyful license. Greco-Roman May ceremonies became mixed with their Celtic, Germanic, or Slavic analogues. The main popular celebration of spring might occur at any time from Lent to the summer solstice, but nearly everywhere, May Day remained the supreme nonreligious festival of spring. Boys and girls went into the woods (so they said) to collect May boughs for decorating houses; to pick nosegays of hawthorn flowers, wild roses, or lilies of the valley; to bring back trees for planting, or more commonly, to cut one for conversion into a Maypole around which they would then dance.

While the Maypole itself was gradually abandoned to finishing schools for daughters of the bourgeoisie, much May Day symbolism survived in the new, revolutionary May 1. In Paris the phenomenon led to an odd class strug-

Paris police bloody heads at a May Day rally in 1891.

gle among the flowers themselves. As far back as 1893 Parisian workers taking part in May 1 demonstrations had decorated their lapels with a sprig of flowering hawthorn, like the village May Day celebrants of former times. A little later, French socialist leaders launched an attempt to replace the hawthorn by the wild rose, no less traditional but presumably more revolutionary because of its color.

Though the hawthorn fought a stubborn delaying action in more conservative working-class lapels, the eventual victory of the wild rose seemed inevitable. Then, just as the tide of revolutionary enthusiasm was beginning to ebb from its 1906 height, the lily of the valley, a special favorite with Parisian midinettes, joined in to make it a three-sided contest. By May Day of 1914 the socialist newspaper *L'Humanité* was able to report that many workers were managing "to marry the wild rose to the lily of the valley in their buttonholes."

During the 1920's there was an increasing tendency among the workers to observe May Day by amalgamating its already traditional political cere- monies with those of a far older tradition, the so-called Lily-of-the-Valley Festival. This "festival" is simply a variant of the usual May Day folk rites. Apart from the coronation of a lily queen, its celebration mainly includes picknicking and hunting for the small, white, bell-shaped flowers in the nearest woods. The custom has seemingly been revitalized by the political May Day—especially since the date became a legal holiday—and recently it has spread throughout a large part of France, reaching into Switzerland.

Wherever the public authorities are cool-headed enough to realize that red flags and Red rhetoric do not necessarily mean Red revolution, and wherever capital and management understand that the worker is no less important to them as a potential consumer than as a producer, it seems likely that the traditional spirit of May Day as a spring rite will prevail over attempts to make it a day of class warfare.

Edmond Taylor, who described the resurrection of Communism's leading unperson, Trotsky, in our Spring, 1971, issue, is finishing a history of colonialism.

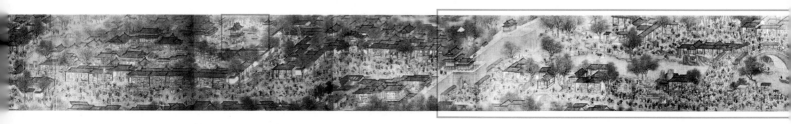

THE RITES OF SPRING

APRIL IN CHINA

(A.D. 1120)

When fair weather finally broke winter's hold
on the Yellow River valley,
a whole great civilization went on holiday.
And a Sung dynasty
painter lovingly recorded every detail

By WALTER KARP

The water-girt pavilion, left, is a detail from the Chinese scroll painting Ch'ing Ming Shang Ho —Spring Festival on the River. *Nearly thirty-three feet long and about the height of a* HORIZON *page, the full scroll is shown in two strips, above and below. Outlined on the bottom strip are both the location of the detail—it is part of an imperial palace—and the portion of the scroll reproduced, overleaf, in a full-scale foldout.*

The Chinese scroll painting known as *Ch'ing Ming Shang Ho,* or *Spring Festival on the River,* of which a central portion is reproduced in the foldout opposite, is surely one of the most remarkable documentary pictures ever painted. Because of it, we know more about the life and look of twelfth-century China than of most other medieval societies—how a twelfth-century Chinese quacksalver peddled his medicines on a suburban road, and what a twelfth-century Chinese restaurant looked like.

Spring Festival on the River does not merely record a festivity; it encompasses, with an encyclopedist's passion for detail, nothing less than an entire civilization as it looked eight and a half centuries ago on its annual springtime spree. It is a painting to amble through —from right to left, in the Chinese manner—following the route of the holidaymaker and taking in the sights that he, too, went to see.

The scroll is a Ming dynasty version of a lost original commissioned around A.D. 1120 by the Sung emperor Hui Tsung, a ruler chiefly remembered for an act of monumental folly: in one year, 1126, he lost half his empire to northern barbarians by stupidly provoking them into invading his realm. Still, Hui Tsung, a lover of the arts, did commission the artist Chang Tsê-tuan to paint *Ch'ing Ming Shang Ho,* for which we have ample reason to be grateful.

Ch'ing Ming, which means, somewhat surprisingly, "clear and bright," is a festival named after the weather, though its announced purpose is to honor the dead—the one major activity that the painter has almost totally ignored. An occasion for universal rejoicing, Ch'ing Ming falls on the 106th day after the winter solstice. In the Chinese reckoning this means around the first week of April, when the inclement winter of northern China suddenly gives way to "clear and bright"—and short-lived—spring. On the day of the festival, all China takes a holiday—except, as a glance at the foldout will show, for those who must labor while others make merry: the keepers of the shops, the suppliers of food, and all the peddlers, hucksters, and mummers who dare not remain idle while millions of their countrymen congregate with a gleam of pleasure in their eyes and a few extra coins in their pockets.

The river of the title, the silted watercourse that flows through almost the entire panorama, is the mighty Yellow River of north China. The great city whose walls are seen at the extreme left of the foldout (opposite) is the Sung capital, Pien-ching (now Kaifeng), which in 1120 was perhaps the most sophisticated metropolis in the world, the rich hub of an empire of some one hundred million souls. The artist's portrayal, however, must not be taken too literally, for what he chose to depict was a generalized imperial city and a generalized yellowish river.

The portion of the scroll shown here sets the viewer down near the center of the panorama and also near the middle of the day, for the scroll is laid out to represent a daylong journey that starts in a quiet country setting at dawn and ends, thirty-three feet away, in another country setting at dusk.

At the point where the foldout begins (facing page 41), the traveling viewer has already left dawn and farm fields behind him. He has made his way along an uncrowded country road and come upon the great silted river. He has seen a rustic wedding and passed a rural Buddhist temple. And he has now reached the suburbs of the capital.

There, near a knoll on the far shore of the river, a crowd of common folk —recognizable by their trousers, the gentry wore robes—enjoys one of the minor delights of a holiday: watching other men toil—in this case, some fishermen. Beyond the knoll a magician on a platform does tricks for an audience that looks a little bored. So early in the day, with so many sights still to be savored, it is hard, perhaps, to hold an audience for long.

Next to the magician a uniform array of tiled roofs marks a compact suburban town. The buildings in Chinese towns were remarkably alike in height and appearance. Even imperial palaces did not try to achieve pre-eminence by towering above their neighbors; they had forbidding walls instead.

The viewer now comes upon the first substantial shops, one selling meat, the second wine—made from grapes, raisins, or dates for rich customers, and from rice for poor ones. Shops like these prospered in the Sung era (960–1279), which saw a huge expansion of commerce and the rise of an ambitious, if despised, merchant class. Some aspects of that Sung commercial spirit— abundantly evident in the scroll—have a distinctly modern air. Among the many shops shown in the painting, there is one, for example, calling itself the "Superior Crockery Shop" and another the "Modern Hat Shop." To the left of the two shops a procession of camels, mules, and coolies brings provisions to the city, for, holiday or no holiday, the citizens of the capital have to eat. Beyond the supply train a crowd has gathered to watch a woman walk a tightrope, while her partner, on the ground, provides a musical accompaniment—a popular entertainment that the robed gentlemen do not seem to consider unworthy of their attention.

On the near shore fewer people are visible, but there is no lack of activity. At the far right, boatmen on a high-sterned vessel are strenuously poling

TEXT CONTINUED ON PAGE 41

HORIZON'S FOLDOUT

The scroll painting Spring Festival on the River *is a treasure belonging to the Metropolitan Museum of Art in New York, by whose courtesy we reproduce a center section in the foldout on the following pages. The scroll should be viewed from right to left. Our reproduction begins with the last section of the foldout (facing page 41), continues on the centerfold, and ends with the section that faces this page.*

TEXT CONTINUED FROM PAGE 32

against the current, while farther up-river, sailors lower the sail of a larger boat. Along the near bank three peasants bring a flock of geese to market as members of a good-sized family, bearing the portrait of an ancestor, head out of town, perhaps to visit the grave of the departed. (This pious procession apparently constitutes the one instance in the panorama of honoring the dead, the ostensible purpose of the spring festival.)

Open the foldout and you will find yourself part of a truly tumultuous scene. The traveler has reached the great market of the city, "the full tide of human existence," to borrow Dr. Johnson's description of Charing Cross in the eighteenth century. On the right, the far bank is dominated by a wholesale grain market, the central depot of the city. Outside, a grain wagon is being unloaded, while in a room off a courtyard at the top of the picture, merchants are weighing out money with which to pay off the shippers.

Along the river front five splendid excursion boats wait to transport their worthy passengers. Apparently they can be rented, for the last building off the grain depot, facing the river, displays a sign advertising boats for hire. Adjoining it at an angle is another wineshop. The next shop in line, containing huge jars, is probably yet another wineshop; the last one deals in olives.

The Chinese are not a notably abstemious people. Dotted throughout the markets and the city, and along the roads, are numerous little food stalls that supply the holidaymakers with a variety of delicacies. Eating is one of the supreme pleasures of the festival, and the Chinese—partly in obedience to ritual but also to sharpen their appetites—have gone without hot food for three days prior to Ch'ing Ming. The Sung capital boasted a number of fine restaurants, and even establishments that specialized in regional cuisines, notably the cookery of south China; all this in 1120, centuries before the West had any restaurants at all.

At the great bridge itself the tide of humanity reaches its flood, and here we might stop and ask what some of the people are up to as they hurry to and fro. If they happen to be the inferior sort of holidaymaker, according to a seventeenth-century Chinese scholar, Chang Tai, they are not doing anything much that could be called worthwhile: "in groups of three or five, they push themselves into wherever there is a crowd. . . . They make noises wherever they go, singing loudly even though they cannot carry a tune and acting like drunkards even though they are sober." That, according to one sniffish gentleman, is what *some* holidaymakers are doing.

To the right along the near shore, a band of peasants hauls on the bowline of the big boat whose sail is being lowered. Just to the left of them, peasants, singly and in little groups, carry wheat or drive pigs to market—perhaps to spend the proceeds then and there. Seated at a table under an umbrella, a fortuneteller plies his trade. There is plenty of competition—and variety—in this line of work: across the river, for example, just to the right of the centerfold at the very top of the picture, another divinator can be seen. He reads men's fortunes in their faces, and displays behind him a tool of his calling: a physiognomic chart.

Let us return now to the near bank, where a small, gazebolike restaurant offers alfresco dining in view of boatmen poling upriver. To the left of the restaurant a medicine vendor hawks his wares from a square stand. The circular picture of an eye he displays announces that he sells potions for good vision.

At this point the traveler has reached the near end of the crowded bridge. At the bottom edge of the painting a sportive group eagerly watches a cockfight, while in the angle of the lumberyard to the left of the bridge, a fortuneteller or letter writer conducts his business. Beyond the lumberyard, passersby have gathered in a ring to watch the show put on by another medicine vendor who is also an impressario. He has hired three men to strut about half-naked showing off their muscles—the result, needless to say, of taking the nostrums he purveys. To their left is a shop selling bows and arrows, and behind it, as if oblivious to the mood of the day, a woman is hanging a coat out on the clothesline.

On the opposite bank, to the left of the centerfold, horses graze in the distance and two men play football before a goodly crowd of spectators. To their left rises another complex of buildings, including a stable for camels and stables for horses, some of which are being bathed in the river, to the delight of several women and their children. Here, the traveler to the city has reached the end of the great market, the first climax of the holiday and of the scroll.

Turning to the reverse side of the foldout (facing page 32), we see the great walls of the capital, separated from the undignified market bustle by a lovely canal crossed by three bridges. Things are a little calmer here. Near the topmost canal bridge a man with a pole is apparently trying to retrieve a lost bird from the upper branches of a tree—the bird's empty cage lies nearby on the ground, attended by a little boy. Piercing the stone walls are two arched entranceways, the Water Gate and the Land Gate, each of them surmounted by a guard tower. Yet the high walls are not entirely forbidding: they have their pleasant aspects. On the extreme left, for example, a barber stands on top of the wall cutting a customer's hair, and there are several cozy little stalls nestled companionably at the foot. Beyond the walls stretch the grounds of the imperial city, the luxurious home of the emperor and court, of wealthy merchants and powerful officials, of all, in short, that can overawe a poor farmer who has nerved himself for the trip to the metropolis. But if that farmer perseveres in his holiday travels, he will find himself once again in the sweet, calm countryside, another Spring Festival behind him and the familiar daily routine of life ahead.

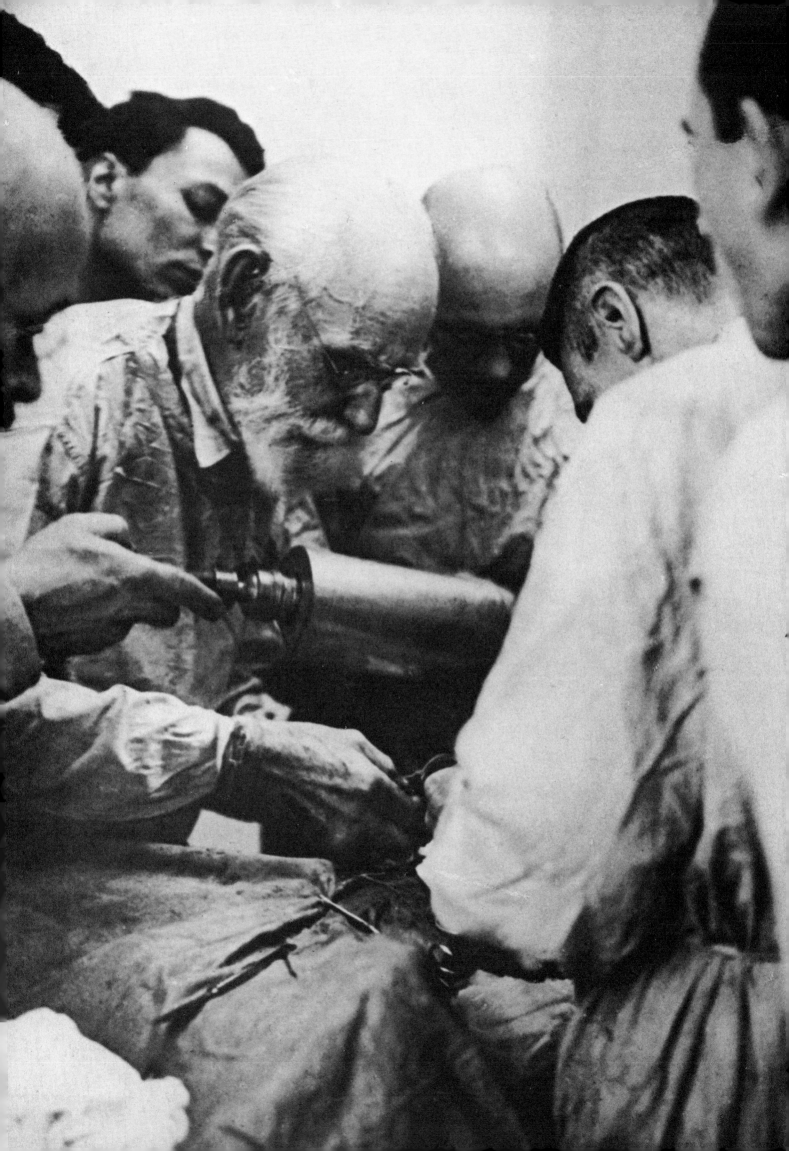

The Pavlovian Century

The rebuilt man need never fear darkness at noon

Joseph Cardinal Mindszenty of Hungary withstood his Communist interrogators for sixty-six hours before he broke. "End it," he gasped. "Kill me!" His body exhausted, his mind disoriented, the cardinal had become a mindless, helpless piece of meat, the victim of a scientific technique distorted and misapplied for political and antihuman ends. The technique is still alive, functioning, successful, and pervasive. It began with the discovery of the classic conditioned reflex by the great Russian physiologist Ivan Petrovich Pavlov. It is evolving into a more Orwellian conditioning, that of "operant behavior" manipulation, espoused today by Harvard's Burrhus Frederic Skinner.

There is no philosophical reasoning behind the classic conditioned reflex. It is a stimulus-response process in which the stimulus may have no connection with the response. Pavlov's dogs heard the sound of a bell and were conditioned to salivate as if for food.

It is B. F. Skinner's theory that the behavior of the living creature "operates upon the environment to generate consequences," though he believes in

The bearded Ivan Pavlov performs surgery on a dog in his laboratory. The discoverer of the conditioned reflex, he searched for the physiological basis of behavior.

reward rather than in punishment during the training period. But in its more lurid forms, operant conditioning *does* use a punishment-reward system and may make men confess to nonexistent crimes—to "generate consequences"— in order to remove the unbearable psychological pressures being applied against them.

The techniques of conditioning, operant or Pavlovian, are having a profound influence today on education, medicine, psychology, and biochemistry. Some of these techniques are coercive, others voluntary, but all may be used to change or modify a man's individual behavior and thus are capable of producing bizarre results in which otherwise intelligent men insist that Communism is democracy, that democracy is fascism, that peace is war, that good is evil, and so on through an Alice in Nightmareland.

Conditioning, no matter what adjective the practitioners care to use with it, classic or operant, has revealed the brain to be an organ of the body that may be regulated like a kidney or manipulated like a leg. The consequences of this knowledge are spreading through the civilized world in a series of ripples sinister to any humanist. B. F. Skinner's recent claim that man can no longer afford to be free and

must submit himself, his behavior, and his culture to outside control for the greater good of the community is, in the opinion of many libertarians, the ripple turned into a tidal wave.

And yet the technique of conditioning did not come from the inquisitional dungeon or from the laboratory of a mad scientist. It originated in the head of a visionary who had a dream of perfecting and dignifying the human race, and who would have been horrified to see any man degraded as Cardinal Mindszenty was in 1949.

Though he was born in the mid-nineteenth century under the reign of Czar Nicholas I, Ivan Petrovich Pavlov was a true twentieth-century man. He was a superb technician who ultimately came to see the human body, including the brain, as a perfectible machine. By studying the machine in motion, as if it were an automobile, he was convinced he could not only reach the central truth of human life but could also make the body and the man function more effectively. Thus, he differed from Freud, who recognized man's limits and understood the price the human psyche had paid for becoming civilized. Freud saw man as imperfectible; Pavlov saw the possibility of a perfect man.

Today, in a kind of sublime confron-

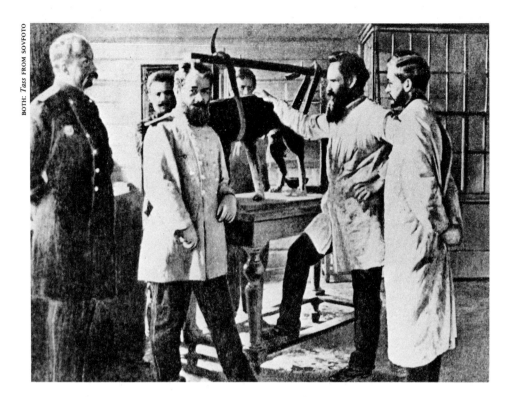

Pavlov, left, rests a hand on one of his experimental dogs as he gathers with his colleagues at the rude Botkin laboratory some time during the 1880's. The diagram above, from one of Pavlov's research papers, shows dogs with holes cut surgically in their stomachs and esophagi, enabling Pavlov to observe their gastric secretions. This experimental technique, which was invented by Pavlov, paved the way for his major discoveries.

tation, these two giants, both seekers of the same truth, face one another across the turmoil of world civilization. Both have transcended their cultures, countries, and centuries. Both have penetrated the East and West. The modern Freudian believes in the uniqueness of man and senses that his full potentialities and limitations are too deep to be easily plumbed. He insists that man's future is unpredictable in the face of the responsibilities placed on him by civilization. The Pavlovian believes in the computer, in the rebuilt man even, who can be governed by chemicals, electric shocks, scalpels, and conditioning.

In the no man's land between these two points of view there is a plastic explosion of rebellious youth and Establishment lawmen, of heart transplants and staggering increases in mental illness, of Chinese loudspeakers blaring slogans into a billion ears and television commercials pushing the hard sell, of the patterning of brain-damaged children and a pill for every psychic pain. Because the world cannot make up its mind whether man is perfectible, Pavlov and Freud presumably must fight it out to the death.

Pavlov is now irrevocably connected in the world's mind with Communist science. He is a peculiarly Soviet scientist-hero, with the politics of his life inextricably mixed with his work. And yet his background, and most of his legitimate international fame, were pre-1917. He was born into a time of profound intellectual activity, a contemporary more or less of Tolstoy, Dostoevsky, Rimsky-Korsakov, Moussorgsky, and droves of distinguished medical men, historians, economists, and chemists. Despite the repressions of czarism and its censorship, the age he grew up in was one of great liberal energy whose pressures, originating in the middle class, eventually wrenched Russia out of its feudal past.

Pavlov was twelve when the serfs won their freedom in 1861. The son of a poor parish priest in the old Russian city of Ryazan, he was indoctrinated—perhaps "conditioned" is a better word for it—to hard physical work in garden and orchard and to an intensive pursuit of scholarship. He always said later that the literature of the 1860's, with its emphasis on objective truth, had turned him to natural science at the university.

The young Pavlov was slender, tall, athletic, his fashionably long beard setting off intense blue eyes and extraordinarily white teeth. His appearance caught the attention of a young woman named Seraphima Kerchevskaya, who eventually became his wife. After the first physical attraction had passed, Seraphima remained transfixed by Pavlov's conversation, by his "hidden spiritual power," as she called it. He did indeed possess the unique quality of genius that would elevate him, regardless of the work he chose to do. This quality was matched by an incorruptible passion for pure truth.

Pavlov rejected the priesthood, his father's calling, and left the seminary without completing his courses. As an undergraduate at the University of St. Petersburg he won a gold medal for his first experiment, conducted with another student. The young men brilliantly described the physiology of the nerves of the pancreas. After he had completed his postgraduate studies at the St. Petersburg Military Academy, Pavlov was asked to work in the physiological laboratory connected with S. P. Botkin's famous clinics.

His "lab" was a bathhouse with no equipment. He had no funds to buy the animals he needed. He had to extract and sell gastric juices (then used for treating human stomach ailments) from his few experimental dogs. He was a physiologist, and no man ever worked harder through the process of physiology to reach his higher objectives. In his farce of a laboratory Pavlov worked on the augmenter nerves of the heart, discovering that these nerves controlled not only the regularity of the beat but its force as well. He married Seraphima in 1881, but as he earned only twenty-five dollars a month in the Botkin laboratory, his family almost starved. His colleagues, worried about the pitiable state of his family, raised some money for him to lecture on the function of the heart. Pavlov gave the lectures, but he used the fees to buy more animals for research. His family got nothing.

His absorption in his work was total. When he failed to receive an appointment to a University of St. Petersburg post that would have solved his financial woes, he was surprised at his wife's bitterness. Did she not understand that the real tragedy of the moment was that his experimental butterflies had all just died?

In a sense, while Pavlov might fiddle with butterflies and measure heartbeats, he was always bound along an irresistible road toward the human brain. As a student, he had studied physiology under I. F. Tyson, a dedicated experimenter. His mind was filled with the electrifying information he had mined out of *Reflexes of the Brain,* the classic work by I. M. Sechenov, the founder of modern physiology in Russia. Sechenov hurled a challenge at both church and state when he said he would attempt "to show the psychologists that it is possible to apply physiological knowledge to the phenomena of psychical life." Traditionalists, believers in the divine mystery of man, all closed ranks against Sechenov, yet for the young Pavlov the book was truth. But to reach the brain offered him by Sechenov, Pavlov had to make an incredibly circuitous journey that lasted nearly thirty years.

It took him until 1890 to achieve some independence of research and a modicum of financial security for his family. In that year he was appointed professor of pharmacology at the Military Medical Academy in St. Petersburg. Five years later, he became professor of physiology at the same acad-

emy. It was a post he would hold for some thirty years.

By all accounts Pavlov was an emotional man. But he became a mechanical monomaniac in his laboratory obsessions, as though, in this other way, he was presaging the century to come. He watched the ballet but his mind was on his work. He always walked fast and did not slow his pace even when walking with his pregnant wife. She miscarried and he overcompensated by carrying her, during her next pregnancy, up every stairway. If he could not win an argument, he shouted his opponent into silence. But he might just as readily apologize.

His impatience was legendary. He believed that every second of time was important. When assistants were doing class experiments for him, he would often leap to his feet and try to speed up the work, sometimes ruining the experiment. Then he would blame the luckless assistant. The students, delighting in these "circuses," would listen until Pavlov's shouts diminished down the corridors of the academy.

In the late nineteenth century the study of digestion was a neglected branch of physiology mainly because most experiments on the intricate workings of the digestive glands killed the animal subjects. Pavlov could not accept this drawback. He maintained aseptic conditions in the operating and recovery rooms so that his dogs would survive surgery. He insisted on dealing only with the functioning animal and was not concerned with classifying dead organs. He thus invented what came to be known as the "chronic" experiment, as opposed to the "acute" experiment, in which the animal died.

Pavlov quickly found that conventional methods of experimentation on anesthetized animals were unsatisfactory. Since anesthetics distorted the reflex action of the nervous system, he used a punishment-reward system to train conscious dogs to lie motionless in their restraint harnesses on the operating table.

This achievement, not duplicated today, was partially helped by his incredible skill and speed as a surgeon. He often worked so quickly that he had finished operating while observers were still waiting for him to begin. He thus broke completely with tradition. Many of his dogs lived on for years, the subjects of countless experiments.

From his early work Pavlov concluded that all blood vessels and organs contained nerves sensitive to mechanical or chemical stimulation. The nervous system, he decided, was the grand regulator of the separate parts of the body, making of them a unified machine. He wanted very much to view his experimental animals as working organisms, and he figured out a way to do it. Early in the nineteenth century a Canadian trapper named Alexis St. Martin sustained an injury that left a permanent hole in his stomach and revealed its workings. Remembering this, Pavlov decided to create his own fistula, or hole, through which he could see the operation of the stomach during the digestive process. He lost nineteen dogs on the operating table before he finally succeeded. He enlarged the experiment by surgically separating one part of the stomach from the other so that he had, in effect, a "control" stomach and an "experimental" stomach with a viewing hole, which came to be known as a "Pavlov Pouch." The pouch had the same nerve and blood supply as the main stomach, and through the hole he was able to view the workings of the stomach's digestive system. Ultimately, using the same technique, he was able to view the workings of the pancreas and salivary glands.

The work on the digestive glands led inexorably to the summit of the nervous system, the brain, and Pavlov understood this clearly. His dogs not only salivated when food entered their mouths, they salivated when he entered the room to work with them, or when they saw food in the distance. Gastric juices flowed in the same way. It was one thing for the body to respond to the taste and feel of food, but it was something else for it to react to what he called "psychic stimulation," where ears, eyes, and nose started physical changes. This put him at the crossroads where he either had to stick to his physiological methods or start thinking about the feelings and desires of his animals.

His resolution of this dilemma was preordained by the nature of his personality. Pure science so dominated his life that he was to dismiss the beauty of Paris, sneer at Switzerland's grandeur, and be bored in Vienna. He was always convinced that Italians washed their hands in their soup.

Pavlov's immense scientific discipline made him a superb technician. But by so narrowing his view, he also limited himself. He would not consider anything he could not see in his laboratory. If criticized for this self-limitation, he needed only to point to the Nobel Prize he won in 1904 for his digestive studies. A humanist or a Freudian might have predicted that research into the psyche, seductive and mysterious as it was, was not likely to appeal to a man who hated Italian soup and Paris.

His decision to follow only the hard and measurable physical facts wherever they were to lead him presaged the Russian Revolution itself. It hinted at the forthcoming transformation of the Russian theocracy into the materialistic society it was to become. "We endeavored," he said, "not to concern ourselves with the imaginary mental state of the animal."

Pavlov had come to his grand realization: if it was possible to examine the reactions of the body to a mental stimulus, then it was perfectly logical to assume one could study what happened in the mind by examining the body. He stood on the threshold of the conditioned-reflex breakthrough. He knew that the state of the external world produced some definite and predictable reactions on the animal. These were the unconditioned reflexes that had remained changeless for thousands, millions, of years. They were the adaptive responses that are built into an organism: flight from danger, migration in season, coughing, blinking. He felt that all animal behavior in an unchanging environment could be explained in physiological terms. Stimulation and response would be automatic.

But the natural environment was full of changes, and Pavlov knew how well he himself could manipulate an artificial environment. To cope with such changes as food scarcity or the onslaught of a hurricane, an animal needed to learn new reflex actions that would allow him to handle emergency situations. What Pavlov now proposed was to turn this learning mechanism into a nearly permanent reaction somewhat similar to the hereditary unconditioned reflex. He would make his dogs salivate when there was *no* food; in short, by using a system of reward and punishment, he would induce conditioned reflexes in his animals in situations where the stimulus had no recognizable affinity with the response, except through the conditioning.

That Pavlov's work on salivating dogs could lead to B. F. Skinner's pronouncement on the end of individual freedom little more than fifty years later is a measure of Pavlov's genius. But between Pavlov and Skinner lies a veritable labyrinth—at least to the layman—of behavioral research. As Pavlov's work was developing in the first decades of the twentieth century, John B. Watson, a psychologist at Johns Hopkins from 1908 to 1920, enthusiastically tried to absorb the principles of the conditioned reflex into his own concept of behavior. Watson, who believed that life responded to conditions set by the external environment, had decided as early as 1919 that a psychologist should be able, if he knew the stimulus, to predict the response. Conversely, if he knew the response, he should be able to specify the stimulus.

Watson was sure that thinking was only a stimulus response, like any other form of behavior. He is famous today, among scientists, as the father of behaviorism in America, and infamous, among humanists, as the man who wrote that if he were given a dozen or so healthy babies, "I'll guarantee to take any one at random and train him to become any kind of specialist I might select—doctor, lawyer, even beggarman and thief, regardless of his talents, penchants, tendencies, abilities."

The route from Pavlov to Watson to B. F. Skinner can be compressed into a paragraph, but it can say nothing of the many intervening years of argument, some of it ferociously bitter, as neobehaviorists grappled with Watson and their own theories of adaptive behavior. It became a morass of complexities as liberal psychologists struggled to handle perception, a subject previously *verboten* because it was presumed to stink of mentalism.

The roadway toward the mechanical man was wide open, but it was also studded with the wrecks of theories. Dr. Horsley Gantt, a lifelong Pavlovian, opened his laboratory at Johns Hopkins in 1932. There, he studied the effects of shock on the cardiovascular system and concluded that trauma, physical or emotional, might permanently damage the system. But even Gantt, who had met Pavlov, finally wrote that "the mind can never be equated with any physical measurement. It can be correlated, but whether it can always be correlated in every detail is open to question."

Meanwhile, for Pavlov, who had elected to travel the physiological road, no such doubts, no wrecks of theories, impeded his work on the conditioned reflex. He cut through the esophagi of his dogs and led both cut ends outside their bodies through the neck skin. This gave him total control over the gastric stimulation of the animal. When the dog ate, the food fell out of the cut esophagus, and Pavlov had a measurable gastric flow. When he actually wanted to feed his animals, he inserted food in the lower part of the cut esophagus. By checking through the hole in the stomach, he discovered that if the animal had not seen or smelled the food, no gastric flow followed. He devised scores of variations on this theme. He would not be hurried. More ebullient theorists, some of them psychologists, seemed at one time to be making faster progress along the path to the mysteries of nervous stimulation, but he limited himself to occasional icy criticism of psychology. All his work was incidental case-history material for an onslaught to be carried out on the brain itself.

All during his digestive and conditioned-reflex experiments, there were dogs who seemed bitterly to resent their fate. They howled, suffered from insomnia, or became agitated in anticipation of the next experiment. Some grew totally unco-operative or panted as though running hard. The heartbeats of others quickened. These were experimental neuroses, accidentally created, but they pointed the way.

Pavlov trained a dog to salivate at the sight of a circle, but not to salivate at an ellipse. Then, gradually, the ellipse was made more circular. The dog, which would be fed only after its correct identification of the circle, began to break down when the ellipse became nearly circular. It howled, bit through its tubes and restraining harness, and barked violently when the experiment was over. It had now, in technical language, decompensated. In this disturbed state, it was incapable of distinguishing between the circle and the ellipse.

During the early, chaotic years of Communist rule over Russia, his belief in man's mutability encouraged Pavlov to continue with his experiments. He worked on two extreme types of dogs: a weak, inhibited type and a strong, lively type. Both dogs were similarly conditioned with six tasks. Then both were systematically broken down by being forced to eat from electrically-charged feeding dishes. This process destroyed the previous conditioned reflexes, making the weak dog sleepy and the strong dog excitable. The quiet dog

ultimately recovered with rest, but the strong dog needed chemical treatment to eliminate his disorder.

A weak type of dog was subjected, in forty-five seconds, to the impact of a gunpowder explosion, a crackle of gunfire, the explosive appearance of a figure in a horror mask, and a sharp movement of the swinging platform to which it was harnessed. The dog went berserk. It became rigid, limbs stiffly extended, head hurled back, eyes staring. Its breathing was stertorous. All its conditioned- and unconditioned-reflex apparatus was paralyzed, and it took two weeks of rest before it could function normally again. A great storm that accidentally flooded its kennel floor brought on another breakdown for the dog later, and this time it took the animal eight months to recover.

All his life Pavlov admired Anglo-Saxon motivation and deplored the Russian lack of it. In the 1920's the Communist rulers were faced with the gigantic barrier of a romantic, erratic, unreliable, feckless people who, given a chance, usually preferred pleasure and vodka to hard work. In the giant bureaucratic structure being built up during those years, Pavlov's work was immediately recognized as important to the state. It proffered, in Pavlov's own words, nothing less than the positive reconstruction of man himself, which from the beginning had been a basic tenet of Communist doctrine. Russia must not merely be united; its people must be remade into a new image. Pavlov and his family, on direct orders from Lenin, were given a luxury apartment and special rations. His laboratory was supplied by the state and in 1924, a new physiological institute bearing his name was built. He was given ample funds and all the staff he needed to continue his work.

Pavlov relentlessly moved along his road, convinced he was very close to the mystery of the brain with his laboratory-induced disorders. He was totally obsessed with his discoveries. His experiments altered glandular functions, causing ulcers and other diseases.

Cardinal Mindszenty led from prison, 1956

Purge judges in the Soviet Union, 1930's

A U.S. soldier broadcasts for North Korea

Pavlov perverted: By applying the principles of conditioning, secret police have devised techniques of manipulation that can turn men into hapless puppets. Victims of such mental torture have included, above: Hungary's Cardinal Mindszenty; Russians led to confess at rigged trials for crimes they did not commit; American war prisoners who denounced their country and "former" selves at the behest of their North Korean captors.

47

B. F. Skinner and his conditioned pigeons

Skinner's daughter growing up in a box

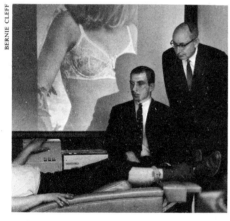

Therapists attempting a cure for homosexuality

Pavlov victorious: Harvard's B. F. Skinner has greatly extended the Pavlovian analysis of behavior in terms of stimulus and response, although it was more for reasons of health than conditioning that he raised his daughter in a glass box. Using conditioning techniques, therapists, above, try to cure a homosexual by giving him electric shocks when pictures of men appear and the "reward" of no shock for pictures of sexy women.

Some of his dogs howled on signal, became disoriented, and recovered. His desire throughout was to cure the diseases he created through what he called "scientifically sound psychotherapy." Eventually, he came to believe that neurotic behavior was caused by straining the nervous system so severely that one or another of its processes broke down, depending on the type of strain and the type of individual stressed. He did not realize that he had set the stage for a tragic drama in which his discoveries were to be relentlessly misapplied.

While disillusioned Marxists were documenting the horrendous mind-destroying techniques of the Soviet secret police, Pavlov moved steadily toward his analysis and understanding of higher and higher forms of nervous activity and operation. His dogs were fed and starved, castrated and loved, overstrained and terrorized, and hypnotized by weak and monotonous stimuli. They had their cortices removed, their thyroid, parathyroid, pituitary, and adrenal functions distorted. The dogs were poisoned to induce pathological changes in the cortex, drugged to intensify inhibitions or excitations, dosed with caffeine to exhaust cortical cells and Veronal to help them sleep it off. It would be unfair to suggest that Pavlov was some unique scientific monster; he did nothing in his laboratory that has not been done untold numbers of times in other experimental situations. His dogs were treated with kindness in excess of anything known in that age. But he lived by the principle that the end justifies the means, and since his aim always was to improve the condition of man, he considered his laboratory simply as a proving ground for theories that might further that goal. In the end he believed that all mental life came out of the fantastically complex physiological organization of the brain itself, although he never found the final proof he was looking for. Simply stated, Pavlov visualized the cerebral cortex as a complicated reception center in which

signals received by the body were broken down and analyzed before being synthesized into new connections and associations. His feelings about psychologists did not warm very much (he was, after all, living in the age of Freud), but he allowed a future for their work if they would co-operate with the physiologists. "I am convinced," he once said, "that an important stage of human thought will have been reached when the physiological and the psychological, the objective and the subjective, are actually united, when the tormenting conflicts and contradictions between my consciousness and my body will have been factually resolved or discarded."

Although Pavlov lived in the shadow of Freud during the latter part of his life, he was steadily being drawn into Freudian territory, albeit unwillingly. He became concerned with the mentally ill and experimented with sleep therapy in a clinic attached to his institute. He dosed his patients with narcotics, kept them in thickly carpeted rooms with heavily curtained windows where a dozen patients might be subjected to slow, blinking blue lights and metronomes beating. Therapists counseled the wakeful. Pavlov found that schizophrenics particularly responded to the rest cure. He felt that the results were "an encouraging and promising start to bringing together experimental physiology and pathology of the higher nervous activity."

By this time he was in his eighties and bore an astonishing resemblance to George Bernard Shaw (who considered Pavlov an imbecile). He was now a totally Soviet man. The cluttered bathhouse had become a gleaming, multimillion-dollar laboratory. A handful of assistants had become hundreds of co-workers. He had been given all the honors of which the Soviet system was capable. A city was named after him, public squares and streets bore his name. In a xenophobic country he could drive a large Lincoln automobile. He was, by any measurement, a giant thinker of the nineteenth and twentieth centuries. And he died in 1936, just as the astonishing confessions began coming out of the Moscow trials.

There is no final method of appraising Ivan Petrovich Pavlov because each year that passes increases the ambiguity, brilliance, horror, and genius of what he started. Perhaps he was merely a vehicle of the times, but more likely he was a prophet. Among modern psychoanalysts, he is respected as the discoverer of the conditioned reflex. Among physiologists, he is recognized as perhaps their greatest pioneer. As one neurophysiologist in New York put it recently: "His techniques are still our crutches, but his ideas are not in our idiom any more."

His weakness, viewed in Freudian terms, is that he lacked subtlety. He was a mechanic, albeit a superb one, but he could not accept the ego since it could not be measured. He never recognized that the ego is capable of raising a series of defenses against conditioning of any kind. "It is," says the New York psychoanalyst Dr. Bruce Ruddick, "a fantastic distortion to think you can change the core of a man's psyche by modifying his responses. Even psychoanalysis, in its concentration, frequency, and depth, is effective for a limited number of people."

A goat can be made to leap over a precipice if you beat him hard enough, but a man may stand there, enduring the pain, rather than make the fatal jump. Man *can* be conditioned, of course, either in the classic, salivating, Pavlovian manner, or in the operant, Skinnerian mold, but the process remains uncertain, faulty, and filled with imponderables. Some American prisoners in Korea confessed to war crimes, but others, with tougher egos and more cohesive social backgrounds, did not. Men in the process of being broken down in solitary confinement, in an atmosphere of threats, rewards, abrupt changes, terrifying events, have kept their equilibrium by counter-conditioning devices—building houses, plank by plank, in their minds, mentally solving abstruse mathematical problems, learning *Paradise Lost* by heart, or by confessing so voluminously to everything that their inquisitors become confused.

In some of today's communes where B. F. Skinner is revered by youngsters seeking cosmos in modern chaos, operant behavior techniques have not been able to do much with rebels or talented individualists. Many of them refuse to conform when their demands are denied, and move on. Conditioning techniques are used every second of the day by behavioral scientists and psychotherapists. A screaming maniac of a child, terrified of eggbeaters, may be quieted by brandishing an eggbeater in front of him. Homosexuals are given an electrical jolt when the picture of a good-looking boy is flashed on a screen, and a comforting massage at the sight of an undressed girl. Some people have been conditioned to regulate their blood pressures and heartbeats.

The Chinese cultural revolution was a gigantic operant conditioning of a large and unwieldy mass of people. Such conditioning, a left-winger might say, is the difference between disciplined, industrious Peking and chaotic, corrupt Saigon. Such conditioning, a right-winger might say, destroys individuality. The political thinkers are in disarray about the conditioned society. Many scientists remain skeptics or are working at conditioning with personal reservations. But there are also many behavioral scientists who agree with B. F. Skinner that operant conditioning is mankind's only hope, even though there is no agreement yet as to how far conditioning can go, or how permanent its effects may be on large communities.

"I have no doubt that society can be conditioned," a New York behavioral scientist said recently. "But do we want to? That is the crucial question."

The layman, bewildered by the complexities and contradictions of it all, may take note of the relentless repetition of television and radio commercials that promise him various "rewards" if he continues to buy and watch. He may be aware of the equally relentless sloganeering by almost everybody—government, the military, minorities—and suspect that this, too, is a form of conditioning. The repetition of certain words and phrases eventually creates an illusion of truth, even if they are lies.

Before Pavlov died, he understood that his road had lengthened as he traveled it. When Wilder Penfield, the great Canadian brain geographer, found that the brain's secrets proliferated faster than he revealed them, he sought refuge in his religion. When Pavlov's son Vsevolod lay dying of pancreatic cancer in 1935, Pavlov told him that perhaps the Communist state was making a mistake in trying to destroy the common people's belief in an afterlife. "The common people need the churches yet for a while. I must write a letter to Stalin," he said.

Pavlov may, in the end, have had his tiny doubts, but our age is Pavlovian. We have found it much easier to put cool white men on the moon than to calm enraged black men on the earth. It is easier to rearrange brain molecules than it is to travel the contradictory road of the metaphysician. If we suppose that Pavlov is right and that man can be taken apart like an automobile and reassembled for another 100,000 hours of useful life, then we have to renegotiate our own contract with being alive. If pleasure comes from the electrode and tears are dried with a drug, we must question the biological purpose of pain and pleasure, and wonder about the ethical usefulness of struggle. We have not heard the last of Ivan Petrovich Pavlov, and he himself, could he have seen the future, might well have had some unconditional comments to make about the quality of his immortality.

Franklin Russell, a well-known writer on ecological subjects and a frequent contributor to Horizon, *is the author of* Secret Islands *and* Searchers at the Gulf.

D. W. GRIFFITH'S
WAY DOWN EAST

This silent film may not be a masterpiece, but it marks
the occasion of a vast cultural change: the fusing of
theatre with film, and the emergence of a new art form

Imagine that a new language has been invented and that, in the first dozen years of its existence, crude sentences are formed with it that only hint at its real possibilities. Then, out of an older discipline, comes a man who seems to have been born a master of the language only recently invented; and he quickly establishes a flexible grammar and a liberating rhetoric. That, approximately, is the role of David Wark Griffith in the history of film.

Griffith was thirty-three when he moved into films in 1908. He had been both a theatre actor and a playwright without much success, which was why he went to work for the Biograph film company in New York—then the center of production activity. When he left Biograph in 1913, he had made about four hundred and fifty films—most of them in one reel, ten minutes or so—and had clarified the new cinema language.

In the next seven years he made seventeen feature-length films. Some of them were very long and complex, possibly because Griffith was reacting against the early restrictions of the one-

When D. W. Griffith wanted an ice floe for Way Down East *(1920), he moved his company to Vermont where he found the real thing. He is shown at White River Junction, flanked by his cameraman, Billy Bitzer (left).*

reeler, and some of them are still peaks of imaginative energy in the medium.

Among these feature films, *The Birth of a Nation* (1915) and *Intolerance* (1916) are the most famous and, justly, the most praised. Lower in this group is the status of *Way Down East* (1920), but for me it is a picture of curious strength and of exceptional interest in American cultural history. I am not attempting here to prove that it is an unappreciated flawless masterpiece; I would like simply to explore the reasons why it is a film to know.

Way Down East was made from a highly successful play of the same name that had its première at Newport, Rhode Island, on September 3, 1897, and that was performed around the United States for more than twenty years. William A. Brady, the producer, recounts in his autobiography how he was brought this play by Lottie Blair Parker, how he thought it had the germ of something but was not in shape, how he engaged an actor-manager named Joseph R. Grismer to revise it (Grismer played the villain in the first production), and how they all wrestled with the script in several versions and through several cool receptions until it became a huge hit.

The Parker-Grismer-Brady play is a melodrama, and came at the end of a century in which the form had domi-

nated the American theatre. What is a melodrama? The term has often been defined—it is one of the easier dramatic terms to define—but for our purposes I will try one more definition. Melodrama is a dramatic form using monochrome characters and usually involving physical danger to the protagonist; its one essential ingredient is earthly justice. A "straight" drama may merely imply justice or may end in irony at the absence of justice; in tragedy, justice is often Hereafter. In melodrama, justice may be slow but it is sure, and it is always seen to be done.

By implication, then, melodrama is an artistic strategy designed, *and desired,* to reconcile its audience to the way things are. In the nineteenth century its chief aim was to support the economic-moral system: a great deal was made of the "poor but honest" theme. (Today, melodrama supports different conventional ideas, like *Mission Impossible* on television.) Many thousands of farmers saw the play *Way Down East* in the years that it toured the country, and they must have known that this Currier and Ives version of their lives was a long way from brute fact, but the fiction gave them two things: escape while in the theatre, and roles to imagine themselves in outside it. As Eric Bentley says, "Melodrama is the Naturalism of the dream life."

By STANLEY KAUFFMANN

Griffith apparently had a sense of these functions of melodrama in a bourgeois, mock-egalitarian society—terms he probably never used. He also must have had some sense of the pluralist nature of the public at any given time, the perception that new interests can coexist with old ones. (For instance, I don't think he would have been surprised that *Easy Rider* and *Airport* were successes simultaneously.) So in 1920, the year in which O'Neill wrote *Beyond the Horizon*, when Stravinsky and Satie were already known composers, when Picasso and Matisse were known painters, two years after the end of a world war that had altered certain traditions forever, Griffith paid around $175,000—much more than the entire cost of *The Birth of a Nation*—for the screen rights to a twenty-three-year-old rural melodrama.

Griffith made many bad decisions in his life, but this time his choice was sound. Lillian Gish, who was to play the heroine, says in *The Movies, Mr. Griffith, and Me:* "We all thought privately that Mr. Griffith had lost his mind . . . We didn't believe it would ever succeed . . . After I had read the play I wondered how I was going to make Anna convincing." It did succeed, tremendously, and in large part because Griffith showed her how to make Anna convincing. Before shooting, he rehearsed his cast for eight weeks in New York. (His studio was then in Mamaroneck, just outside the city.) He had had plenty of experience in the theatre, a theatre that was full of plays like this: he had begun acting in 1897, at the age of twenty-two, with a stock company in his native Kentucky, had struggled in a number of other stock and road companies, and had written a melodrama that had been produced, unsuccessfully, in Washington, D.C., in 1907. Out of this experience, evidently, came the conviction that he knew how to make *Way Down East* "work" and that the postwar public had not shed all its old affinities. And, very clearly, he also understood how film was taking over the form and function of melodrama from the theatre and expanding it in the directions toward which it had been moving.

That's the last point to note before we discuss the picture itself. Inventions don't happen at random in human history. Edison didn't just wake up one morning and say, "Today I think I'll invent the motion picture." Inventions are the result of scientific progress, of course, but also—which is less often recognized—they are often the result of intense cultural pressure. In an invaluable book called *Stage to Screen* A. Nicholas Vardac has shown that "a cinematic approach" was increasingly evident in the popular theatre of the nineteenth century. One can say, not too fancifully, that cultural dynamics foretold the arrival of the film, that the nineteenth-century audience *demanded* that the film be invented.

Griffith was not the only director to understand how the film could satisfy certain hungers in the theatre audience, but he was exceptionally well equipped to take advantage of the metamorphosis. *Way Down East* was not the first, or last, theatre melodrama to be filmed, but, through it, one can almost hear Griffith saying to the audiences of twenty-five years before, "Here! This is what you *really* wanted."

Today it may be necessary to explain the title. "Down East" is an old phrase used to describe the farthest reaches of New England, particularly Maine, which at its tip is considerably east of Boston. The picture tells the story of Anna Moore, a poor and innocent country girl who goes to visit rich relatives in Boston and is there seduced by a wealthy womanizer, Lennox Sanderson. He has his way by tricking her with a false marriage. He asks her to keep their marriage secret for a while, but when she becomes pregnant, she asks to be recognized publicly as Mrs. Sanderson. He reveals his trickery; she goes off in solitude to have her baby, who dies soon after birth.

Anna is turned out by her censorious landlady, takes to the road, and eventually comes to Squire Bartlett's farm. She asks for work. The squire is at first reluctant to hire her because she is unknown and may be immoral; but, persuaded by his wife and son, he engages her. Anna proves her virtue by hard work (how else?), and the squire's son, David, falls in love with her. When he declares himself, she tells him, without disclosing the reason, that nothing will ever be possible between them.

Sanderson's country estate is nearby, as it happens (as it *has* to happen). He discovers that Anna is on the Bartlett place, and he urges her to move on. She tries to obey—he still has "male" power over her, evidently—but the Bartletts, who know nothing of the Sanderson matter, although they know him, persuade Anna to remain.

Some months later, at the end of winter, the secret of her past comes out. She is sent forth into the night by Bartlett, but not before she reveals that Sanderson, who is an honored guest at the squire's table, is the guilty man. She wanders through a snowstorm, faints on the ice of the river just as it is breaking up, and is almost carried over a falls, but is rescued by David. Sanderson then offers to marry her authentically; she refuses. She is forgiven by the squire, because she was tricked into immorality, and in the end she marries David.

Many have noted the resemblance of this story to Hardy's *Tess of the D'Urbervilles*. Whether the authors of the original play knew *Tess*, I don't know. It would not have been necessary: the materials were not all that original, even for *Tess*. The difference with Hardy lay, among other reasons, in the fact that he was not interested in demonstrating justice. But Griffith knew Hardy's work, at least in filmed form. In a 1917 interview he said: "Somehow, most of the stars who come to us from the regular stage lack sincerity. . . . Mrs. Fiske, in *Tess,* was a notable exception. I know she drew from me the tribute of tears." It may be that three years later he was remembering that "tribute," and it helped him to decide

Meeting her inevitable fate, Anna Moore (played by Lillian Gish, center) is ordered out into the night by Squire Bartlett (Burr McIntosh).

to film this somewhat similar story.

There are a number of subplots involving other characters, and it is worth noting that, in the original typescript of the play, each character has a casting tag: "Martha Perkins, Comedy Spinster; Hi Holler, Toby Comedy," and so on. (A Toby was a rustic clown who usually bested smarter city folks. Until quite recently Toby shows toured the Midwest.) *All* the characters are theatre stock, both in the sense of platitude and of availability, a method of show-making at least as old as the *commedia dell'arte.*

Griffith engaged a playwright named Anthony Paul Kelly to do the screenplay and paid him ten thousand dollars, but, says Miss Gish, Griffith retained only one thing from the Kelly script: a bit of comic business with her

gloves and elastic tapes that always got a laugh and so, to Griffith, was worth Kelly's entire fee. The screenplay that was used, presumably Griffith's own, is a model of the film adaptation of plays, in the sheerly technical sense. Much of the formal beauty of play design arises from limitation: the necessity to limit action and to arrange necessary combinations of characters on stage. The skill with which these matters are handled can be a pleasure in itself, as well as a positive enrichment of the drama. But this skill is not essential to the screenplay, which has infinitely greater freedom of physical and temporal movement, can unfold intertwined material into serial form, and can run virtually parallel actions. These contrasts can be seen in the Parker-Grismer script and in Griffith's

screenplay—in principle. (I don't want to magnify in the slightest the literary worth of either.)

Griffith begins his story chronologically, with Anna's visit to Boston. This gives him several advantages: he can show the homes of the rich, thus visibly dramatizing the difference between sophisticated city life and country simplicity; he can give Anna the experience of betrayal and loss of her child "on stage"; and he can make her a differently seen character by the time she reaches the point of what was her first entrance in the play. When she first appears in Squire Bartlett's farmyard in the play, a wanderer looking for work, we soon understand that she has some sort of secret; but at that same point in the film, we know her history— we are already her confidants and she

Fleeing headlong across the snow, Lillian Gish worked tirelessly for Griffith in sub-zero weather as he shot the stormy finale of Way Down East.

is already a heroine. However, Griffith had the problem of establishing the Bartlett home and his male star before Anna reaches them—about half an hour into the story. He solved the problem with a device deliberately borrowed from Dickens. He inserts the title "Chapter Two . . . Bartlett Village" at an early point and gives us glimpses of the farm and David (Richard Barthelmess), relying on our assumption that if he's not insane, he's showing us these scenes for a purpose that will become clear. In fact, the lack of clarity is itself an enticement.

Griffith links the two strands before Anna and David meet with mystic prescience; for instance, when Sanderson drops the wedding ring during the mock marriage, David starts suddenly from sleep in his bedroom. (No ex-

planation of why David is in bed during the bright day of the mock marriage not so many miles away!) This mystic device, sentimental as it is, simultaneously draws on three kinds of design protocol: that of the theatre, of the novel, and of the purely cinematic, fusing them into a new form that we can call the film.

The most obvious physical expansion is in the storm scenes at the end, which were filmed over a considerable period of time outdoors in Mamaroneck, New York, and in Vermont. There is also a shot of Niagara Falls. (In one Mamaroneck blizzard we can see snow gathering on Miss Gish's eyelashes. And in her autobiography she tells of floating on a Vermont ice floe so long that her hair froze and her hand, trailing in the icy water, felt as

if it "were in a flame.") The advantage in excitement of this physical expansion is self-evident; it is the realism, or purported realism, that, as Vardac shows, the Victorian theatre was aching for. But also, on the thematic level, it gives us a much more engrossing way of sharing Anna's purgation.

Still, in recognizing the advantages provided by the film form, we mustn't lose sight of what theatre practice meant to *Way Down East*. As a result of his own stage experience and viewpoint, Griffith patently relied on verity of acting to sustain the picture, and indeed the best acting moments are the film's anchor points today. The truth of those moments, in a script that is beneath serious regard, stands out like the best arias in a trumpery old opera.

The remarkable fusion of new film

elements and old theatre heritage is why *Way Down East* is still effective and why it is historically important. On the one hand, we see Griffith using sheerly cinematic language to fulfill his drama. When Sanderson (Lowell Sherman) is introduced, there is a quick succession of cuts—close-ups and medium shots—so that his first appearance sparkles prismatically, dangerously. When he and Anna first meet, we see him over her shoulder before we see them together, as Griffith uses the film's power to shift the audience and thus increase the feeling of encounter.

When Anna is thrown out by her landlady after her baby's death, there is a lovely long-shot of her starting down a country road, her few possessions in a box under her arm—a shot that bitterly contrasts the beauty of the scene with her sorry condition. (Usually Griffith uses nature shots to endorse a character's feelings; this contrast is an exception.) She arrives at the Bartlett gate on foot, and Griffith intercuts a shot of Sanderson on horseback, at his estate nearby, thus commenting sardonically and at the same time knitting his plot. When the spinster Martha Perkins discovers the facts of Anna's past and hurries to spread the gossip, we get one of the film's few tracking shots: the camera trundles ahead of her on the snowy path and—a crucial element in film aesthetics—its very motion becomes part of the idea of the scene.

Further, the seminal influence of Griffith on other directors can be traced to this film as well as to the usual sources, *The Birth of a Nation* and *Intolerance*. The early Soviet masters, in particular, responded to it. Sergei Eisenstein writes at length of the background of *Way Down East* in his essay "Dickens, Griffith, and the Film Today." V. I. Pudovkin writes in *Film Technique* that in the storm sequence the harmony between the blizzard and Anna's feelings "is one of the most powerful achievements of the American genius." Pudovkin adapted the metaphor to his own purposes in

THE CUT

In a sequence that is still perfectly hair-raising (all the more so because Griffith used neither stunt men nor camera tricks), Richard Barthelmess as David (1) rescues Anna from the ice floe on which she has fainted (2). Cutting masterfully from one face to the other, Griffith shows Barthelmess struggling across the icy river (3), the beautiful Miss Gish in a swoon (4), the pair about to be swept over the waterfall (5), and the final leap to safety (6), just in the nick of time.

his film *Mother* (1926): the breakup of the ice is used there as a larger symbol —of revolutionary turbulence—but it clearly owes a great deal to *Way Down East* in vocabulary and technique.

On the other hand, we can discern the fruits of Griffith's purely theatrical gifts. Some instances: the handling of Barthelmess so that, quite soon, his very movements articulate the poetic qualities of his personality and quicken his trite role; Anna's face, as Sanderson tells her that their marriage was fake; Anna in the discovery of her baby's death; and, an even keener theatrical touch, the very next scene in that bedroom, where the bereft Anna is sitting on a stool next to the rocker in which she had baptized her child and gently rocks the now-empty chair. Talk about the "tribute of tears!"

Possibly Griffith's highest achievement here as director of actors is the ballet he created with Lillian Gish's body. If there were no titles of any kind, one could "read" her body: the butterfly dance around her little parlor as she awaits her supposed husband; the crushed figure who trudges the road after her baby's death; the recovery of some self as she works at the Bartletts—a medium between the joy of the beginning and the desolation of the abyss. She tells us, simply by the way she moves around the Bartlett place, that she will never again be as happy as she once was but at least she is once more breathing. Since Miss Gish did her best acting for Griffith, it seems fair to assume that her fine performance closely reflects his direction.

1.

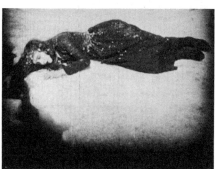

2.

3.

4.

5.

6.

1.

2.

3.

4.

5.

6.

THE CLOSE-UP

Lillian Gish's performance as Anna is an enduring delight; the mobility of her face makes the spoken word unnecessary. This sequence begins as she toys happily with her wedding ring (1) while her presumed husband launches into his confession: they are not married at all. The smile fades (2), then the full shock hits (3, also enlarged opposite). Frames 4, 5, and 6 complete Miss Gish's transformation in a few deft moments from childlike and innocent bride to wronged and frantic woman.

No appreciation of *Way Down East* should lead us to the film-buff silliness of hailing it as a transcendent artwork. It is a mechanical and saccharine story, with dialogue to match, full of blatant moral signals (for example, only bad or frivolous people smoke cigarettes), and Griffith's heavy editorial comments.

What is more, the best print of the film I have seen contains errors of editing (overlapping action, repeated in successive shots), and the light in the storm scenes varies widely. (Some sequences in the original prints were hand-tinted; the absence of that color now may cause those variations of light.) There is even a split second in which an actor seemingly gets a hint from off-camera: the charming Mary Hay catches her heel in her hem and someone, unseen, tells her so.

Still, the empirical fact is that despite all we know about the film as we watch it, it grips us. Substantially this is because of the elements analyzed here, all underwritten by the utter seriousness with which Griffith took the whole project.

And that seriousness is rooted, consciously or not, in the myth that underlies much of melodrama: moral redemption by bourgeois standards. It has been suggested that Anna is a secular saint, truly good, suffering for the sins and blindness of her fellows, finally undergoing an agony that reveals her purity. She is betrayed in her trust, she goes through travail, she labors in humility, she declines happiness because she is unworthy (refusing David's love), and she shows that death holds no terror for her. At last she achieves heaven—*on earth.*

To extend the analogy, the God in the story is the squire (the owner of the Eden)! It is he who at first is about to expel Anna from the Garden, who finds largeness in his heart to let her remain on trust, who at last provides the crucial forgiveness—because when she sinned, she did not know it; she thought she was behaving rightly. Not only is she forgiven, but when she marries David, she wears white; her virginity has been restored by dispensation of the squire. Here, in capsule, is sainthood founded on respectability, which was possibly the chief criterion in nineteenth-century society.

Scoff as we may, the possibility that there *is* earthly justice is the fundamental appeal of *Way Down East,* as it is in our contemporary melodramas. Other old melodramas of stage and screen have died because their claptrap dates and strangles them; this film lives because, beneath and through its claptrap, it makes the possibility of justice poignant still.

And it lives, too, because it is one of the most lucid instances of a tremendous historical change: the theatre culture of the last century being transformed into the theatre-film culture of this century. *Way Down East* feeds on the earlier culture and seeds the later one. In chronology it came fairly late in that historical process; but in crystallizing that process, it is a landmark.

Stanley Kauffmann is film and theatre critic of The New Republic *and visiting professor at Yale.* Figures of Light, *his second book of film criticism, is now in a Harper Colophon edition.*

(*Way Down East* can be rented in its original silent version, uncut, from the Film Department, Museum of Modern Art, 11 West 53rd Street, New York, New York 10019. It is available in 16 mm. ($45) and 35 mm. ($90). Versions with music track added are also available here and elsewhere; only the uncut silent version is recommended.)

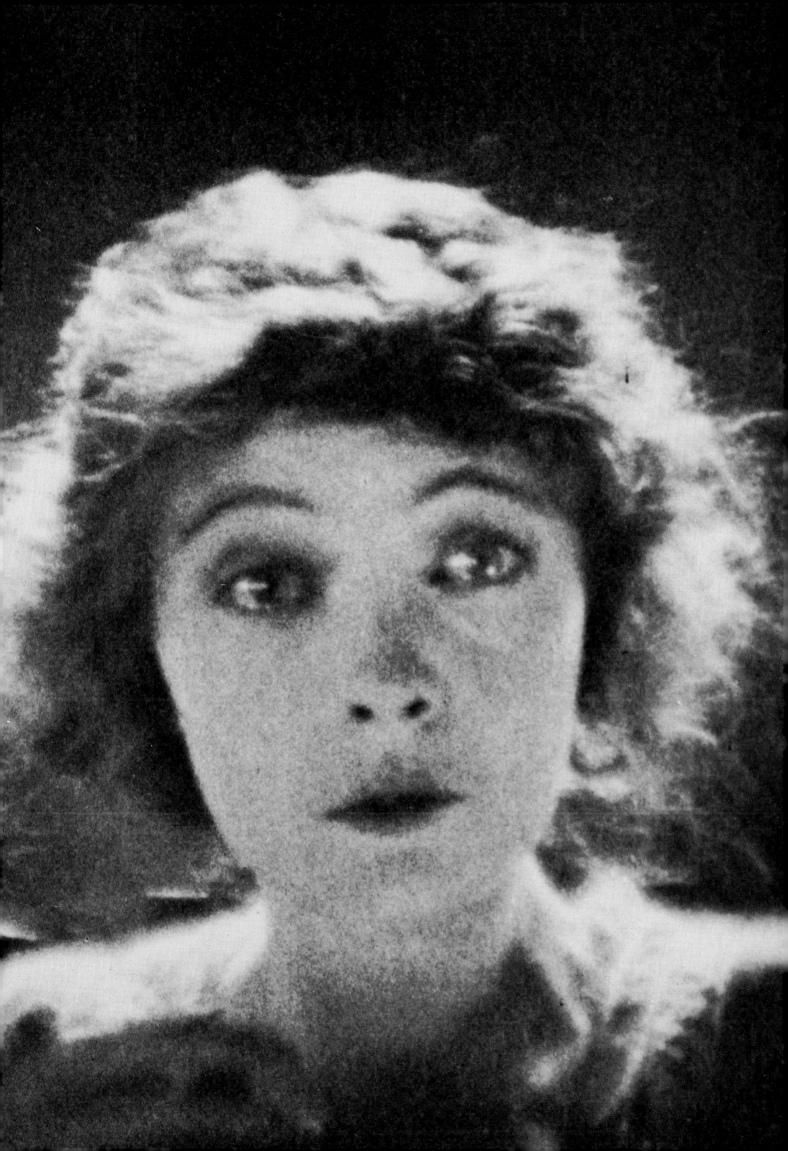

"To awake. To die. To be born"

Guru Gurdjieff in 1924, hiding his charisma under a fur hat

With these words G. I. Gurdjieff came as close as he ever did to explaining how to acquire a soul. To this end his followers gladly sacrificed energy, time, money—even their lives. Today his bizarre teachings are finding new favor among the young

By KENNETH CAVANDER

There you are—in a fine mess.

With these words to his pupil, Georgi Ivanovitch Gurdjieff, carpet seller, mystic, and author of *All and Everything*, a work considered by some to be the first true anti-Bible since *Thus Spake Zarathustra,* died. It was October, 1949.

For more than thirty years Gurdjieff had been provoking contradictory and sometimes violent reflexes among the intelligentsia of two continents. Katherine Mansfield and Frank Lloyd Wright were devoted to him; D. H. Lawrence and Sigmund Freud made fun of him. For some of those who met him the experience was the most significant of their lives; for others, it was the most ominous. Mysteriously rich, he demanded cash payment for even the slightest service; enormously attractive to women, he was corpulent, often coarse in his manner, and completely bald. He was called Prophet, Messiah, Savior, Grand Lama; he was also called a Rasputin, a Beelzebub, a twentieth-century Cagliostro. Who was this man, and what was the source of his unnerving effect on people?

Modern civilisation is based on violence and slavery and fine words. But all these fine words about "progress" and "civilisation" are merely words.

In such sweeping indictments, Gurdjieff contemptuously dismissed the culture of the West. According to him, modern man is a machine, devoid of a soul. "Can a man who is the product of contemporary civilisation and education do anything at all himself and by his own will? No!" Gurdjieff's scorn for material values and his ingenious adaptation of Eastern mystical techniques gave him a strong appeal to the generation that survived World War I. Today his words are finding a new and wider audience. *All and Everything* is still in print, and Gurdjieff's face stares from dust jackets of several books to be found alongside the latest best seller or sex manual.

G. I. Gurdjieff was born in Russia,

of Greek descent, and spent his childhood in the Caucasian town of Alexandropol. (The date of his birth is one of the many facts about himself that he kept secret, but it must have been about 1865.) His father was a wealthy peasant, fallen on hard times, who became a carpenter and in the evenings told stories for the entertainment of his neighbors. Hearing these stories, says Gurdjieff, "all my childhood games were enriched by my imagining that I was someone who did everything not as it is usually done, but in quite a special way."

Hearing legends about gods, devils, and fairies, seeing traveling shamans, gypsy fortunetellers, dervishes, cases of miracle healing and possession, Gurdjieff grew up impatient with the conventional wisdom taught at the seminary he attended in Alexandropol. "There exists," he reasoned, "a something else, which must be the aim and ideal of every more or less thinking man, and it is only this something else which may make a man happy and give him real values, instead of the illusory 'goods' with which an ordinary life is always and in everything full." And so Gurdjieff, while still in his twenties, set out to track down this "something else."

On his travels he earned his living "in quite a special way"—as a maker of artificial flowers, a carpet seller, a restaurant owner, a mender of phonographs, a seller of "American canaries" (ordinary sparrows dyed rainbow colors), a dealer in oil wells and fisheries. He wandered all over the Middle East and Central Asia, sometimes accompanied by a few friends called the "Community of Truth Seekers." The little band traveled through Tibet, the Hindu Kush, Turkestan, the Gobi, always trying to piece together the essential doctrine behind all great religions and philosophies.

Twenty years passed—years that remain largely unexplained. In his semi-autobiographical *Meetings with Remarkable Men*, Gurdjieff hints only at the first steps in the search that eventually took him into seclusion, as the pupil, perhaps, of a group of "secret masters." The exact source of his teaching will probably never be known. All that is certain is that in 1914, or a little before, he reappeared in Russia. There, in a small café in an obscure part of Moscow, he was introduced to a Russian intellectual and journalist, P. D. Ouspensky, who was to become his pupil, his rival, and finally, his Boswell.

"I saw a man of an oriental type," writes Ouspensky, "no longer young, with a black mustache and piercing eyes . . . this man with the face of an Indian raja or an Arab sheik . . . in a black overcoat with a velvet collar and a black bowler hat, produced the strange, unexpected, and almost alarming impression of a man poorly disguised, the sight of whom embarrasses you because you see he is not what he pretends to be . . . He spoke Russian incorrectly with a strong Caucasian accent."

Though skeptical at first, Ouspensky left Gurdjieff's presence with the feeling that he must meet this man again. Whatever Gurdjieff had learned in his travels, he gave others the impression that he had found what he was seeking. And now, in his mid-forties, he was ready, he said, "to actualize in practice what I had taken upon myself as a sacred task"—no less than the awakening of Western man.

To awake. To die. To be born.

Through this aphorism Gurdjieff expresses virtually his entire philosophy. But in order to awake, one must first "remember oneself," and the concept of self-remembering is one of the most difficult of all the puzzling ideas in Gurdjieff's teaching. Even the philosopher and mathematician Ouspensky, an expert in handling abstract ideas, found it hard to define; after a great struggle, he concluded that it meant "directing attention on oneself without weakening or obliterating the attention directed on something else." When a student complained that it was impossible to "self-remember," Gurdjieff would answer, "What else do you want? People who know this already know a great deal . . . If a man really knows that he cannot remember himself, he is already near the understanding of his being."

What made Gurdjieff's system so exasperating at first to Ouspensky, and to all lovers of logic, was the ruthless way in which he destroyed their first halting attempts to understand it. This was deliberate, for Gurdjieff despised the overintellectualization of Western man. "You must feel, you must feel, your mind is a luxury!" he would shout. "Never think of results, just do!" He wanted to dismantle the human machines he saw around him and create men. To this end he gave his pupils a series of "shocks," intellectual and emotional, designed to break them of their mechanical behavior.

Every meeting with Gurdjieff led Ouspensky into greater complexities; the system into which he was being initiated has, in fact, filled several books and defies summary. Gurdjieff himself did everything in his power to prevent it from becoming a system at all, and when pupils quoted his sayings back to him, he would often brush his own ideas aside as rubbish. Nevertheless, some themes kept recurring. Gurdjieff believed, for instance, in three centers, or "brains," in man: the intellectual, the emotional, the moving-instinctive. In most people these three centers are at odds; Gurdjieff proposed to show how they could be brought into harmony. One step toward this is self-remembering; another is to stop what he called "identifying"—forming emotional attachments to objects, words, ideas—and to stop "considering"—caring about the opinions and prejudices of others.

Pupils also were expected to perform complicated exercises, derived from sacred dances Gurdjieff had witnessed during his travels. Meanwhile, the pupil was to make difficult arithmetical computations in his head, while his emotions were brought into play by the repetition of a phrase such as "God have mercy!" Then, in the middle of a movement, Gurdjieff would shout "Stop!" and everyone had to freeze, holding his position if he could or dropping to the floor if he could not, until the Master cried, "Enough!"

Many of the techniques Gurdjieff used are familiar to psychotherapists; others are age-old devices of psychic conditioning and personality control. In his lectures and anecdotes he drew, often word for word, from Sufism, Buddhism, Vedanta, Yoga practices, dervish dances; but he usually transformed them in some personal way. Reaching people at a time of confusion and despair, these ideas, derived from the Eastern tradition of inner wisdom and detachment and transmitted through Gurdjieff's abundant energy and imposing logic, struck many intelligent people as a revelation.

When Ouspensky met him, Gurdjieff was commuting between groups of followers in Moscow and St. Petersburg. But the Russian Revolution was approaching. With magnificent indifference to the surrounding chaos, Gurdjieff continued to teach, but eventually he was forced to collect a few disciples, Ouspensky among them, and take refuge in the small town of Essentuki, on the Black Sea. There he conducted intensive lectures, discussions, exercises, and trials of endurance, setting out every aspect of his system in its main outlines. It was during this period that Ouspensky began to have doubts about Gurdjieff, doubts that were strengthened over the following months and finally led to the separation of the two men.

Meanwhile, the civil war was spreading. In 1918 the group disbanded, and Gurdjieff went on to Tiflis, taking a few disciples with him. In Tiflis he continued his work in a changed form, giving public lectures and preparing some sacred dances. Once again, however, the group was forced to move,

and after a succession of stops—Istanbul, Dresden, London—Gurdjieff finally entered France, raised the money to make a down payment on a château outside Fontainebleau called the Prieuré d'Avon, and opened the Institute for the Harmonious Development of Man.

"I was not very enthusiastic about the program of the Institute," writes Ouspensky, who had by that time broken with Gurdjieff and settled in England. "I realized, of course, that . . . G. was obviously obliged to give some sort of outward form to his work having regard to outward conditions . . . [but] this outward form was somewhat in the nature of a caricature."

Was it, though? The Russian composer Thomas de Hartmann, who stuck by Gurdjieff all through the travels in Russia and Europe, disagrees emphatically: "Mr. Gurdjieff consistently followed the same line of work from the time we met him in 1917, although he always dressed it, so to speak, differently." Caricature or not, the institute at Fontainebleau became a mecca, during the next decade, for all sorts of people: White Russian émigrés, dissatisfied intellectuals from England and France, doctors, psychiatrists, artists, American socialites, curious ex-Theosophists, young and gifted people with no settled aim but a yearning toward the supernatural. Some came for a week or two, others for a few months, a handful for years.

So long as they stayed at the Prieuré, disciples were under a strict regime. Orders for the day were posted each morning. A famous doctor would clean out the cowshed; a poet would chop wood for the furnace that would heat the Turkish bath being constructed; an American heiress would hoe the herb garden. And at the end of the day everybody would be called upon to perform the exercises, listen to lectures, and prepare for an exhibition of the sacred dances. Rehearsals took place in the "study room," a large hall built by the students from parts of an old air-

craft hangar. It was decorated with Oriental rugs, lighted by windows on which elaborate patterns were painted, and contained a special box in which Gurdjieff would sit to watch the performances.

In those early days at the Prieuré, a student would go to bed at two or three in the morning and rise at six. No one could escape Gurdjieff's lash: "You all dirt!" he would shout at them. No one was allowed to reach a plateau and stay there. The more advanced you were, the more you were expected to do. And then, into this atmosphere of enthusiasm, frenzy, chaos, and exalted dreams, came the thirty-four-year-old Katherine Mansfield, in full expectation, so she said, of a cure for the tuberculosis that was destroying her lungs.

"There is so much life here that one feels no more than one little cell in a beefsteak," she wrote to her husband after her arrival at Fontainebleau. This was in October of 1922; the institute was young, and much work remained to be done on the property. Miss Mansfield was spared any serious exertion, but Gurdjieff, after giving her a luxurious room on the main floor ("the Ritz," he called it), later moved her to a poky little den that was always cold. She wore her fur coat night and day, but was grateful for the lesson because it taught her how little she really needed in order to live. And soon afterward, in one of his unpredictable reshufflings of the rooming arrangements, Gurdjieff put her back in her opulent quarters. Three months later, she died of a hemorrhage of the lungs.

The death of the gifted and famous writer brought down the wrath of the Establishment on Gurdjieff and his "Forest Philosophers," as the press called them. Gurdjieff was accused of luring Miss Mansfield there at a time when she might have been receiving medical care that would have prolonged her life. On the other hand, his supporters argued that she was doomed anyhow, and the experience at least made her last months happy. From her letters it is clear that she went of her own free will; but whether she would have recovered elsewhere, or been happier under an ordinary doctor's treatment, no one can say.

In spite of the unfavorable publicity that came out of the Katherine Mansfield episode, glowing reports from Gurdjieff's satisfied pupils had brought him more students than he could accept. In 1924 he made a lucrative trip to the United States, during which the sacred dances were performed at Carnegie Hall, and it was rumored that he returned richer by $100,000. Groups had been started in this country under the supervision of A. R. Orage, editor of the *New Age*, an influential literary magazine, and back in France the Prieuré was in good running order. Gurdjieff bought himself a powerful new automobile, and for all his students—bicycles. Then, driving his car fast one night on the road from Paris to Fontainebleau, he lost control, careened off the road, and struck a tree. Though severely injured, he somehow managed to crawl out of the wreckage, cover himself with a rug, and lie in the road until a passing gendarme found him. For five days he remained in a coma; when he regained consciousness, the Institute for the Harmonious Development of Man heaved a collective sigh of relief.

Gurdjieff now turned his full attention to writing. Every day, at his favorite café in Paris or on the grounds of the Prieuré, he dictated a manuscript, in Russian and Armenian. For years this manuscript was only brought out to be read aloud by pupils under his watchful eye. A few carbon copies were circulated among favored pupils, and in the early 1930's an attempt to raise money was made by selling the copies for fifty dollars each. Occasionally, a rich American would be allowed to pay for the privilege of leafing through some pages—one lady is said to have paid a thousand dollars to look

through twenty. In time, this mysterious book achieved almost the status of a religious relic, until, in the last months of his life, by one of those abrupt reversals for which he was famous, Gurdjieff gave instructions for the manuscript to be published. In 1950 the mystery was exposed in print.

It turned out to be, of all things, a space odyssey.

It was the year 223 after the creation of the world, by objective time calculation, or as it would be said here on the "earth," in the year 1921 after the birth of Christ.

Through the universe flew the ship Karnak *of the transspace communication . . . On the said transspace ship was Beelzebub with his kinsmen and near attendants.*

So begins *All and Everything*, one of the most grandiose and infuriating philosophical works ever composed. This colossal book (it runs to 1,238 pages) was written "to destroy mercilessly the beliefs and views of the reader, by centuries rooted in him, about everything existing in the world."

Gurdjieff advised his readers to read each of his "written expositions" three times before trying to fathom the gist of them. It was good advice. He despised what he called the "bon-ton" style and wrote with an Oriental elaboration that, at least in the translations made by his pupils, gives his arguments the intellectual equivalent of the design on a Persian carpet. A single sentence runs as follows:

Now when in the new part of these "two-natured" formations everything corresponding was acquired, and when all that functioning which is proper to such cosmic arisings to have was finally established, then these same new formations in their turn, on exactly the same basis as the first case and also under the conditions of a certain kind of change of functioning, began to absorb and assimilate into themselves such cosmic substances as had their arising immediately from the Most Most Holy Theomertmalogos, and similarities of a third kind began to be coated in them which are the "higher sacred parts" of beings and which we now call "higher being-bodies."

Gurdjieff himself, at the sessions where his pupils read the book aloud (it *does* sound better that way), would give synopses of the meaning of each passage and roar with laughter at the jokes he had inserted. In fact, the joke is on the reader who tries to make deadly serious sense out of every last word. *All and Everything* is a brilliantly contrived maze, part deliberate deception, part comic extravaganza, part profound mystical philosophy. Gurdjieff's own judgment of it was simple and blunt: "Epics will be written by men who have understood something in 'Beelzebub.'"

The book is cast in the form of a series of conversations that take place between the chief passenger on the spaceship, Beelzebub, and his favorite grandson, Hassein. Beelzebub is often a mouthpiece for Gurdjieff, and Hassein (the reader?) is treated as a bright but naive child. Characters include "our ALL–EMBRACING–ENDLESSNESS" and "the Chief-Common-Universal-Arch-Chemist-Physicist Angel Looisos"; the narrative describes such cosmic laws as the "sacred Heptaparaparshinokh," as well as a history of the earth from the time the moon was torn adrift from it by the pull of a passing comet. Beelzebub discusses subjects as diverse as the riddle of the Sphinx, polygamy in Persia, and American food; he also talks about his six incarnations on earth, in which he was disguised as a mortal man and earned his living at various professions. At the end of the space journey Beelzebub is rewarded for his labors and promoted to a higher state of being.

All and Everything was meant to be a preparation, not a final statement of Gurdjieff's philosophy. That was to follow in later volumes, one of which has been published as *Meetings with Remarkable Men*. The third part, said to be entitled *The World is Only Real Then When I Am*, has not yet appeared.

The dictation of his books, the debilitating effects of the accident, the exhausting work with pupils—all these took their toll. The situation was not helped by his uncompromising and—some thought—brutal treatment of individuals and groups who taught in his name. Reproached for one especially lacerating verbal attack on a disciple, he was asked why he bothered with such people in the first place if he was later to repudiate them so violently. Gurdjieff is said to have replied: "I needed rats for my experiments."

The depression came. The finances of the Prieuré went from bad to worse. Gone were the rich Americans, the English intellectuals, the White Russians with their family jewels. In 1933 he brought a Paris banker to see the institute, and took him on a tour of the crumbling property. Gurdjieff discoursed grandly on the limitless possibilities of the place, on the pupils who would come. The banker listened, and as he left he was heard to mutter, *"pas possible."*

The following year Gurdjieff sold the Prieuré, and the Institute for the Harmonious Development of Man, one of the most ambitious experiments in raising man by his psychic bootstraps ever attempted, was closed forever.

Gurdjieff was nearing seventy, though no one knew his exact age. "He's been saying he's eighty-three ever since he stopped saying he's forty-five," said a pupil who knew him in Paris. From then until his death, fifteen years later, he became a familiar figure to the people of the *quartier* around la rue des Colonels-Renard. *Le marchand de bonbons* they called him, because his pockets were always stuffed with sweets, which he lavished on the neighborhood children. But he still had other "goodies" to dispense, and from all over the world people sought him out —for the same reason as always, in the hope of acquiring a soul.

Gurdjieff's table became itself a form of philosophy. He had a storeroom crammed with the most exotic foods to be found in Paris, and his meals were lengthy toast-filled marathons, in which the various categories of "idiot" received attention. He would ask the guests to which category they thought they belonged, and if the guests could not answer, he told them. Sometimes only two or three would be invited; at other times, such as Christmas, as many as sixty people would squeeze into the small, antiquated apartment, whose shutters seemed permanently closed against the light.

One thing did not change—the enigmas that trailed him like shadows. People who came to see him during this period saw either a corpulent, slightly seedy Russian Armenian with a stained waistcoat, who smiled a little too much and a little too broadly and affected an arrogantly cryptic manner, and about whom stories circulated of his insatiable sexual appetites; or else they felt themselves to be in the presence of a man who scrupulously measured their spiritual weight and was unsparing yet respectful of their individuality. All agreed on one thing, however: Gurdjieff was a master trickster who could assume any character at will. Even his towering rages seemed to be a deliberate act, from which he himself stood a little apart, watching to see what effect they would have on their audience.

In 1948 he paid another visit to New York, where he arranged for the publication of *All and Everything*. There he read the manuscript of Ouspensky's account of the early years in Moscow and the Caucasus. Ouspensky had been dead for some time and the estrangement between the two men had become complete, although it had softened somewhat toward the end of Ouspensky's life. But now, after reading the pages of *In Search of the Miraculous*, Gurdjieff remarked, "I hear myself talking," and the book was published with his approval. Back in Paris in 1949, he once again was in a car accident, but miraculously (he was in his eighties) recovered. In October, however, he began to weaken, and as the first half of the twentieth century drew to a close, his disciples learned that G. I. Gurdjieff was dead.

Gurdjieff was, for good or ill, one of those rare beings—a Master. What a Master *says* is less important than what he *is*. He teaches by *being*. What there was to be learned from Gurdjieff could probably be learned best by contact with the man, by rubbing against his presence until the friction produced a spark that would ignite something in the other person. Gurdjieff was, in other words, an alchemist of the soul, creating heat by which the coarse spiritual body could be transmuted into gold; but like the alchemists of old, he needed a little bit of gold in the other person to begin the Great Work. In fact, a generation before C. G. Jung published *Psychology and Alchemy*, Gurdjieff had pointed out the spiritual significance of the medieval alchemist's quest for the arcanum, and the metaphor of transmutation through fire, heat, or cooking often appears in his teaching.

Fusion, inner unity, is obtained by means of friction, by the struggle between "yes" and "no" in man. In order to make further development possible he must be melted down again, and this can only be accomplished through terrible suffering.

Today, more than twenty years after Gurdjieff's death in la rue des Colonels-Renard, the reverberations of his words and thoughts still disturb people. "Do you want to die like dogs?" he would shout at his pupils when he thought they were lazy or backsliding. To such a question only one response is possible. That is why the groups he started or inspired still meet and enroll new disciples; why the sacred dances he introduced to the West are still performed in esoteric circles; why books about him, as well as his own extraordinary writings, are still sold steadily.

The Western world, meanwhile, is still in a fine mess. And quite a few people today believe that Gurdjieff was offering mankind a practical way to clean it up.

A GALLERY OF GURUS

A s the 1920's had their gurus—Gurdjieff, for example—our present decade, not to be outshone in matters spiritual, has its own. What is a guru? A religious teacher who has seen the light and leads others to it. The idea of guruship and discipleship is common to most of the religions that have recently sprung up in the United States: Yoga, Zen Buddhism, Sufism, Hare Krishna, and the other cults that have come to us out of Asia via California. Peter Rowley, the author of a report called *New Gods in America*, estimates that American followers of Oriental faiths, together with scientologists, satanic cultists, Gurdjieffians, Black Muslims, and other home-grown anchorites, must number about two and one half million. Before we are all washed away in this metaphysical monsoon, HORIZON hastens to present a selection of up-to-the-minute gurus, photographed—where else?—in California.

The smiling guru on this page is Katagiri Roshi ("Roshi" is a transcription of the Japanese term for Master), second in command of the Zen Center in San Francisco and of the Tassajara monastery, situated on a mountaintop in southern California. The disciplines of Zen are dauntingly rigorous. Katagiri's students must seek enlightenment through *zazen*, which is usually translated as "just sitting." About sixty men and women, at last report, live at Tassajara, all of them disaffected young Americans. Meat, drugs, and alcohol are forbidden; bouts of hard labor alternate with bouts of *zazen*. Reveille is at four o'clock in the morning. Full-time residence, however, is not a requirement.   S.T.

PHOTOGRAPHED FOR HORIZON BY TONY RAY-JONES

Inhalation and Meditation

Seekers for spiritual improvement who are unequal to the demands of Zen may wish to follow a simpler path, and Janardan Paramahansa, shown above blessing a new disciple in San Francisco, can show them the way. This octogenarian is Master of the Ajapa Breath Foundation, with forty thousand adherents in India and an unspecified number in America. According to the leaflet issued by the foundation, "Ajapa Breath is the most ancient method of breathing." Ordinary breathing, says the guru, results in a net loss of energy to the breather, and "this imbalance is harmful for Man and disastrous to the World." Ajapa Breath, on the other hand, creates "a thrust in the out-going breath which increases the inhalation (in-coming breath)." Lessons in this technique cost ten dollars each and last half an hour. Janardan travels from coast to coast and averages twenty new students per day. His headquarters, presently located in Montreal, provide additional guidance by mail.

Master Subramuniya, who appears opposite in a traditional Hindu meditation pose, is the founder of a far-flung institution called the Wailua University of Contemplative Arts, with campuses in Alaveddy, Ceylon; San Francisco; Virginia City; Nevada; and Honolulu. The curriculum stresses meditative arts and Shum, a new language that describes the niceties of mystical experience. A native Californian, the Master likes modern methods: much of his teaching is done via cassette recordings, communication between campuses is by teletype, and there is a computer in the Honolulu office. Discipleship is not limited to men, nor to celibates, but women cannot become nuns until age fifty. Young men of the order are often trained to be waiters—"the silent ministry" as the Master calls that profession. Wailua U. is not for the impecunious; the school workbook retails smartly at fifty dollars; trips to Switzerland and other mountain retreats run to about $1,500.

Spiritual Summit Conference

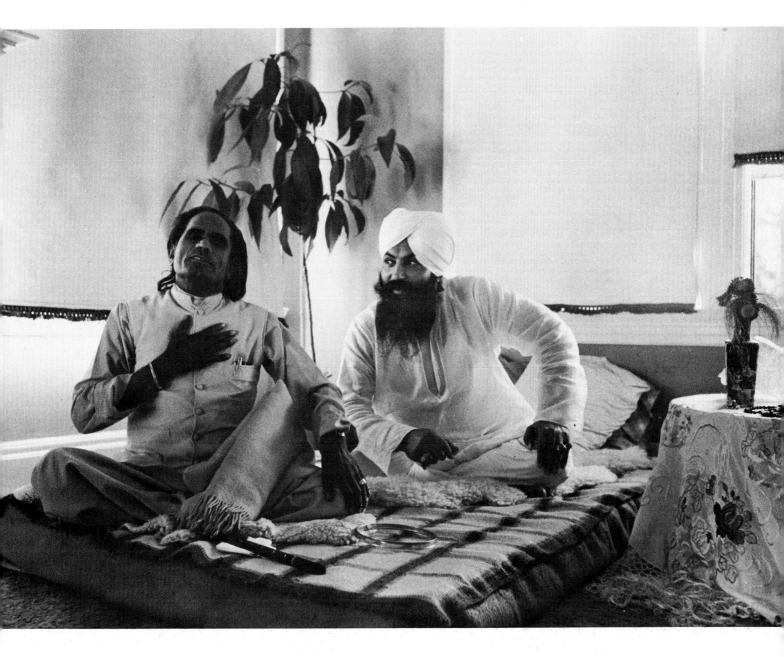

The guru opposite, encircled by his devotees, is known simply as "Father." He lives in San Francisco with fifteen women, whom he calls his goddesses, their various children, and three male disciples. He is head of the Foundation of Revelation, which had its beginnings in Calcutta in 1968. A leaflet published by the foundation relates that in October of that year, while in Calcutta for the Spiritual Summit Conference, five Americans—"Shotsy, Patty, Sheyla, Don, and Buz"—spotted Father in the guise of a beggar and followed him home. After numerous adventures, they managed to transport their guru to Berkeley. Shotsy the fortunate owner of a "speedy Porsche car," took him in tow, and eventually, says the leaflet, he "was reported in the society column in the famous Vogue magazine." Now comfortably established in his commune, he is recognized "by men of thought," he says, as embodying considerable knowledge and cosmic power.

"I have seen God. It is a light equal to millions and billions of rays of sunlight," says Yogi Bhajan, who is shown above, at right, with Dr. Rammurti Mishra, a colleague visiting from London. Yogi Bhajan runs an ashram, or monastery, in Los Angeles and is said to have 100,000 American disciples. He also directs a group known as 3HO (Healthy, Happy, Holy Organization), which helps to propagate the faith. According to a 3HO brochure, Yogi Bhajan "is a spiritual revolutionary, aware that the science of yoga has been abstracted and polluted in the Western World and he has come to teach correct methods of physical and mental conditioning which will allow students to experience a real contact with the Divine Forces within." Yogi Bhajan's enlightening technique involves "uncoiling the coiled energy under the navel point, raising it through the spinal column and injecting this energy into the pineal gland, which has been described as 'the seat of the soul.'"

"What Is It For?"

The goal of all spiritual paths is *ananda*—joy or divine bliss. Such is the credo of Swami Kriyananda, the happy guru in the photograph above. He owns a tract in the foothills of the Sierra Nevada in northern California, called the Ananda Meditation Retreat—"72 acres [it is now 320 acres] of rolling terrain, covered by pine, cedar and oak trees . . . The views are expansive . . . The sun, when out, is always warm." Seventy people live in this paradise, each family in its own geodesic dome, wigwam, or cabin. As with all things, the search for *ananda* has its price: admission to the retreat is $1,000, and then one must build one's own home, as well as enroll in the Self Realization Correspondence Course at a fee of $250 a month. Service is $65 monthly, but one may economize on drugs, alcohol, and meat, all forbidden. The swami is an accomplished vocalist and composer. His record albums include "Say 'YES' to Life!" and "What Is It For?"

Kennett Roshi, who appears opposite flanked by two monks, is an Englishwoman, born Peggy Kennett forty-eight years ago in Sussex. She is a full priestess of Zen Buddhism, having been ordained in Malaysia a decade ago, as well as the abbess and official missionary of a Zen temple in Japan and the founding director of Shasta Abbey, a training monastery in northern California. She has some thirty students, male and female, married and single, whom she directs in meditation and in the labors of building and running a retreat. After five years students are expected to return to the ordinary world "to make use of their new-found peace and serenity . . . for the benefit of themselves and the people with whom they work and live." Harried by a 10 per cent mortgage on her property, Kennett Roshi cannot accept as many students as she wishes and often must solicit donations. Current needs: a cement mixer, a large bell, and a very large Buddha.

Oldenburg Draws
Seven New Wonders
of the World

Claes Oldenburg aims a devilish eye on the world around him, transforming whatever he sees into weird creations that may keep their original shapes but mysteriously lose their old identities. He started out in this amazing business ten years ago with his happenings and continued it with his pop art sculptures. This same wizardry is still at work in the monuments he is currently dreaming up—among them the "Seven New Wonders of the World," a series of imaginary colossi drawn by Oldenburg especially for HORIZON and here presented for the first time.

Harold Rosenberg of *The New Yorker* has called Oldenburg "the liveliest artistic intelligence to emerge in the United States for the last ten years," and to critic Barbara Rose he is "the single Pop artist to have contributed significantly to the history of form." Even those who object to the sense of comedy lurking about his works are unable to write him off merely as a jokester. As John Canaday of *The New York Times* observes, "After all, W. C. Fields and Robert Benchley were gagmen, humorists and entertainers. The thing that saves Oldenburg is that his work is consistently humorous at a very high level."

To art lovers who are afraid he is kidding, Oldenburg suggests that they simply "assume that it is a very, very serious proposition."

By choosing ordinary objects without any aesthetic associations as subjects for his sculptures and monuments—a toilet, a typewriter eraser, an ice bag—by making them bigger than life, and by using unexpected materials and textures, he forces people to see their inherent forms from a brand-new angle. He also sometimes discards from familiar items the parts he considers nonessential, leaving only what interests him: the laces, eyelets, and rubber toes from a pair of gym shoes, the round ears from Mickey Mouse, a detached human knee, a sliced-off ear, an isolated navel. He also changes their natural substance—banana into plaster, car into canvas, bomb explosion into coral—and may turn them into ominously powerful objects a hundred stories tall (see page 77 for the monumental toy bear) or half a mile long (see pages 78–79 for the giant saw bridge).

Oldenburg at work is the same alert collector of ideas as Oldenburg at leisure. "I have a thing about ears," he says, and he is like an ear himself, always attuned to the idea he knows is dormant in, say, a typewriter eraser, a teddy bear, a subway map. His mind contains hundreds of compartments to store such treasures as the light flowing out of a flashlight, or the water shooting out of a drainpipe, or the dishes sliding out of a dishwasher—each waiting to be turned into an object or a monument. Oldenburg lives and works in lower Manhattan in a pair of five-story commercial buildings joined by various passageways. He goes from one high-ceilinged sunny studio to another, tending numerous projects, much as he tends the ideas in his mental compartments.

"I fear being only one thing," he says, so he becomes many. Early in his career he opened a store in Manhattan, selling plaster cake and fruit he made in a back room, thus becoming artist and merchant at the same time. Since the merchandise sold from between $49.95 and $499.95, the project was a notch above playing store. Today most of his energies go into planning his "colossal" monuments. "At the moment I am pretending to be an architect," he says. "I think that it is because the artist doesn't have any real place in society that I assume a

By ROY BONGARTZ

Claes Oldenburg poses in his New York studio with one of his characteristic works—an outsize plastic handsaw.

position that does have some reality, like an architect. Or maybe the artist does have a place and I'm just thinking that I don't have one."

Oldenburg probably acquired his odd perspective of himself and the world in childhood. He was born in Sweden and lived there and in New York until the age of seven, when his family moved to Chicago, where his father was Swedish consul. Not knowing any English, Claes felt isolated, so he invented a make-believe country, Neubern, an island in the South Atlantic: it had fully-mapped cities, population figures, flags, airplanes, and armies. Meanwhile, his aunt back in Sweden sent him collages of magazine illustrations to decorate his room. She did not concern herself with proportion, and as a result, a photo of a slice of bread might be larger than that of a man. One of these collages shows an adding machine, an old-fashioned stand-up telephone, a fountain pen, an ink bottle, a pair of dice, a samovar, some sardine cans, and a Burroughs typewriter—figures that have recurred in Oldenburg's work.

Until he was about fifteen Oldenburg lived a secret life in Neubern and was an all-American high-school boy at the same time. He next studied acting at Yale University, then was a police reporter in Chicago, and for a couple of years wrote poetry. After studying at the Art Institute of Chicago, he began to concentrate on drawing. His most frequent model was a girl named Pat Muschinski, whom he married in 1960. (They have quite recently been divorced.) She appeared in many of his happenings, which put people and odd, heterogeneous objects into sometimes jarring confrontations. For one of these, he got the loan of a brand-new cement mixer; of the cement mixer Oldenburg said at the time, "It's almost like lion taming, dealing with technology this way."

In 1962 he staged in his East Side store a series of ten happenings for which he made a lot of props. After an art collector bought two of these—a couple of stuffed canvas boats—for $650, Oldenburg began to make the now famous plaster sandwiches and ice-cream cones that launched the pop art era. Aided by his wife Pat and other admiring ladies eager to serve as seamstresses, Oldenburg turned out an impressive line of drooping vinyl bathtubs, eggbeaters, toasters, juicers, shoestring potatoes, scissors, electric fans, and typewriters. Then, in 1965, his vision expanded by a new 200-foot studio, he began to design his colossal monuments. Paradoxically, these work out best drawn on a small scale; the eye of the viewer can encompass a small space more easily, and thus, Oldenburg believes, the impression of hugeness is more emphatic.

Claes Oldenburg is not putting anybody on; if there is duplicity in his work, it arises from the contradictory nature of his ideas. The joke, if any, is not really meant to be funny. Oldenburg still lives partly in Neubern, partly in New York, and such schisms show up in other ways in his personality. "I live a hermetic life," he says, "because I am always communicating. I alternate between an absolutely private life and an active outside one; I retreat to make a sculpture and then I have to come out in order to present it." Contradictions are what Oldenburg loves most; he sees them everywhere. There is the real and the false, the hard and the soft —he greatly enjoys reading the lists of antonyms in *Roget's Thesaurus*. "I have formulated an expression of nature in terms of opposites." Such expression could consist, for example, in depicting a naturally soft object—

TEXT CONTINUED ON PAGE 81

71

The Seven Wonders

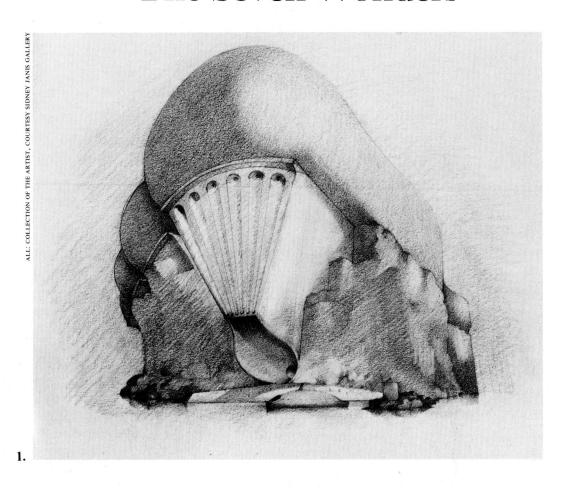

1.

1. *Planned Monument to the American Indian,* above, consists of a huge left foot, sole skyward, surmounting the sheer rock of Alcatraz Island. The fan-shaped structure extends up from the entrance to the nail of the big toe. Seen from a plane, the monument would look like the foot of a man buried head-down—"a very positive statement about footprints," says Claes Oldenburg, and perhaps about the Indians as well.

2. *Cemetery in the Shape of a Colossal Screw,* opposite, was inspired by a news story about the shortage of burial space in São Paulo, Brazil. Oldenburg's screw-shaped cemetery would rise thirty stories above the city streets. When it was filled, it would be screwed into the ground, leaving behind at street level a circular restaurant built into the screwhead.

3. *Memorial to the 1941 Attack on Pearl Harbor, Hawaii —Water "Park" with Foliage,* overleaf, consists of massive rocks and coral rising out of the harbor in the shape of furious clouds of smoke. To Oldenburg, the silence and tranquillity of his petrified explosions make an appealing contrast to the real raid.

4. *Tower in the Form of a Colossal Thumb,* Oldenburg's imaginary gift to the Soviet Union, a veritable colossus

of roads, is based on an old tale about a czar who was mapping out a new highway. His thumb got in the way of his pencil, causing the line to jog; the imperial engineers carefully included this error in the finished plan. Besides serving as a symbol of the absurdity of despotism, the glassed-in thumbnail would house a restaurant. Oldenburg has a thing about restaurants.

5. *Colossal Sculpture in the Form of the Bear on the Flag of California* depicts the bear upended and, in this sketch, in the final stages of excavation from the side of a hill. His feet rest upon the monumental equivalent of the grass shown on the actual flag.

6. *Bridge over the Rhine at Düsseldorf in the Shape of a Colossal Saw* is Oldenburg's answer to his own question, "Why should buildings not have the shape of objects?" The giant saw bridge would be made of steel with a glassed-in arcade running through the teeth. A passage above would carry vehicular traffic.

7. *Arch to Span the Suez Canal* consists of two huge columns joined by a slender span and each surmounted by a replica of the Sphinx's ear. The columns would serve as listening posts, one to be manned, or eared, by Israelis, the other, of course, by Egyptians.

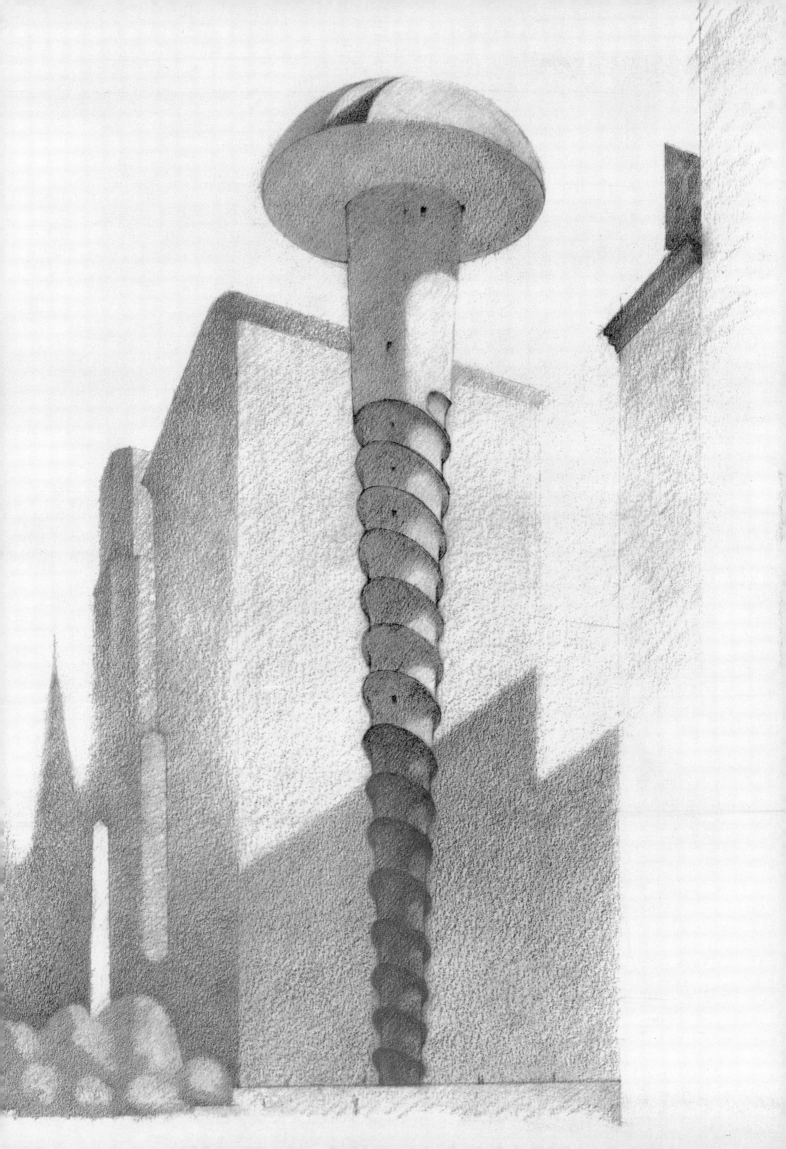

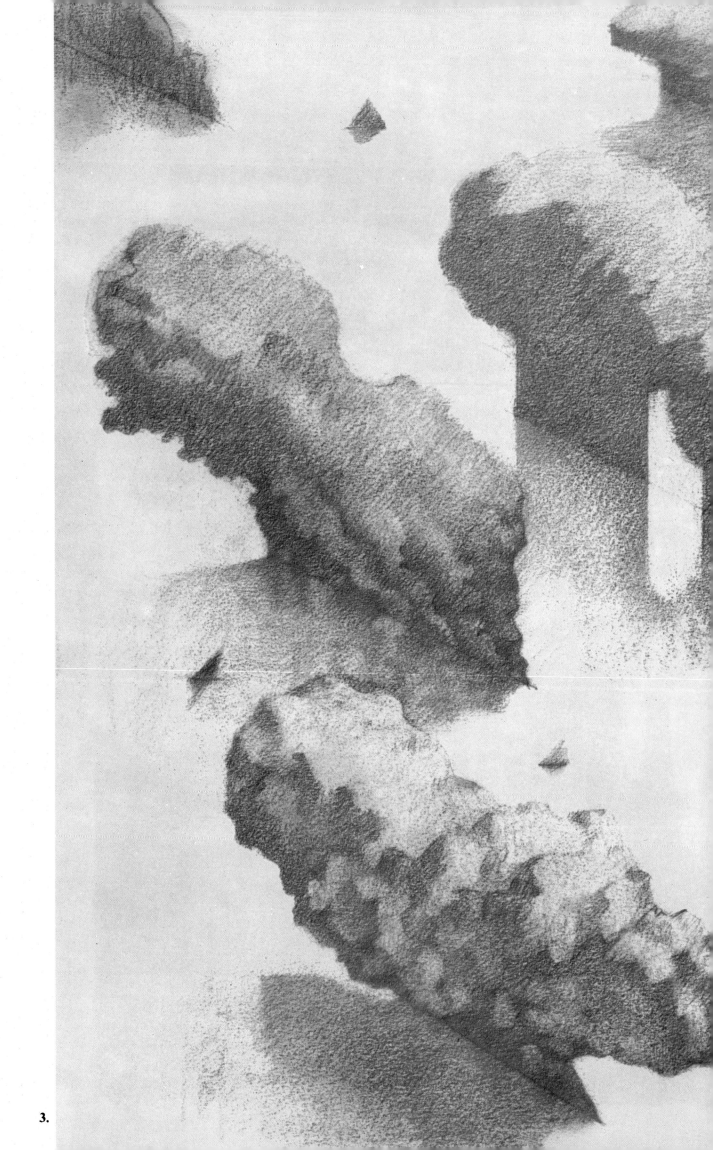

3.

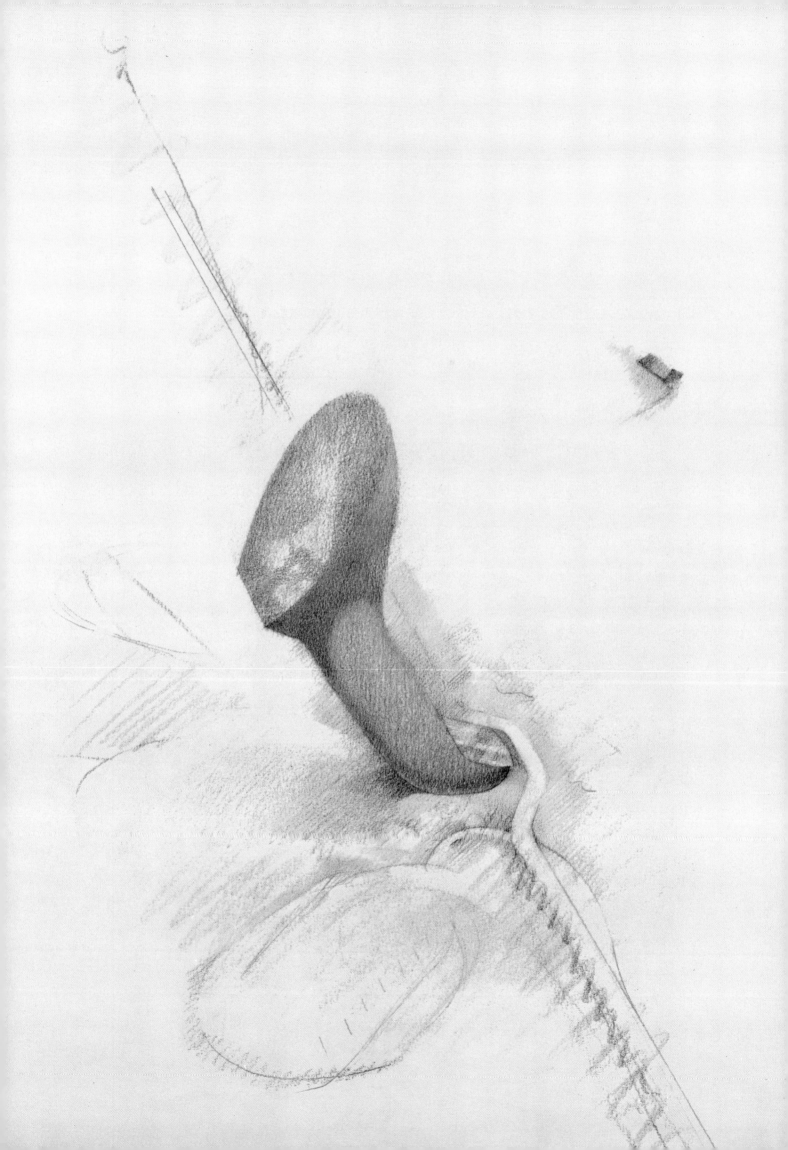

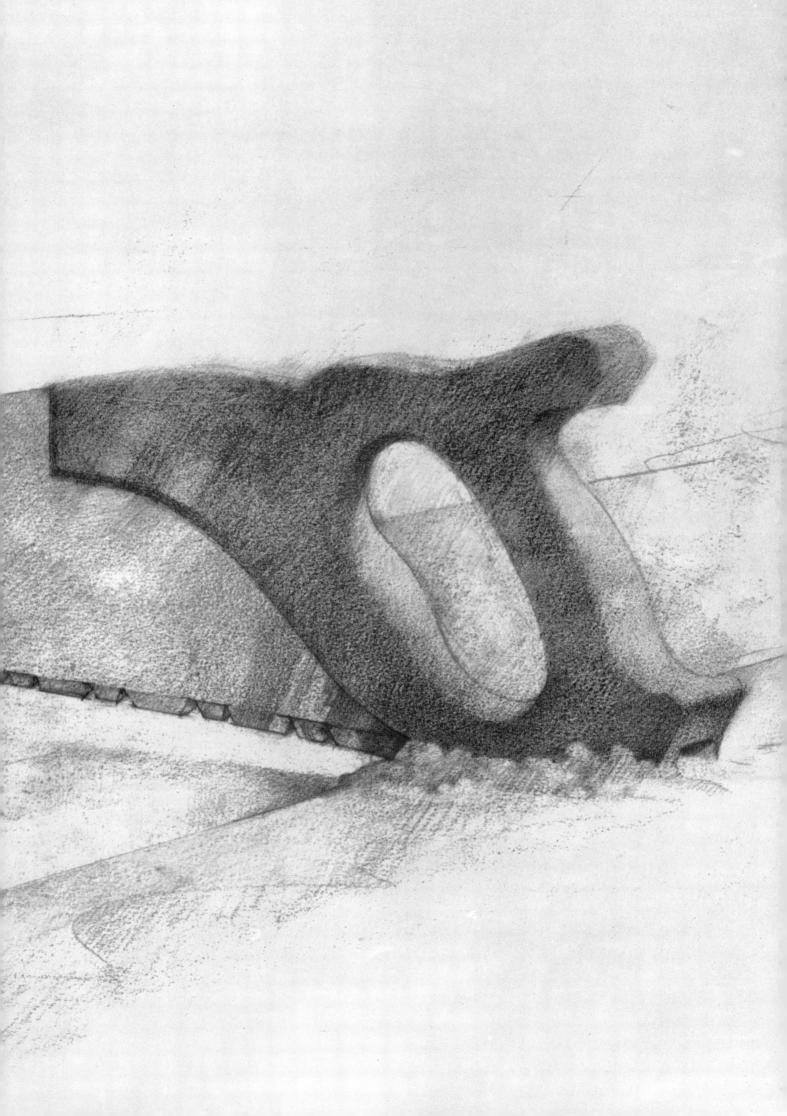

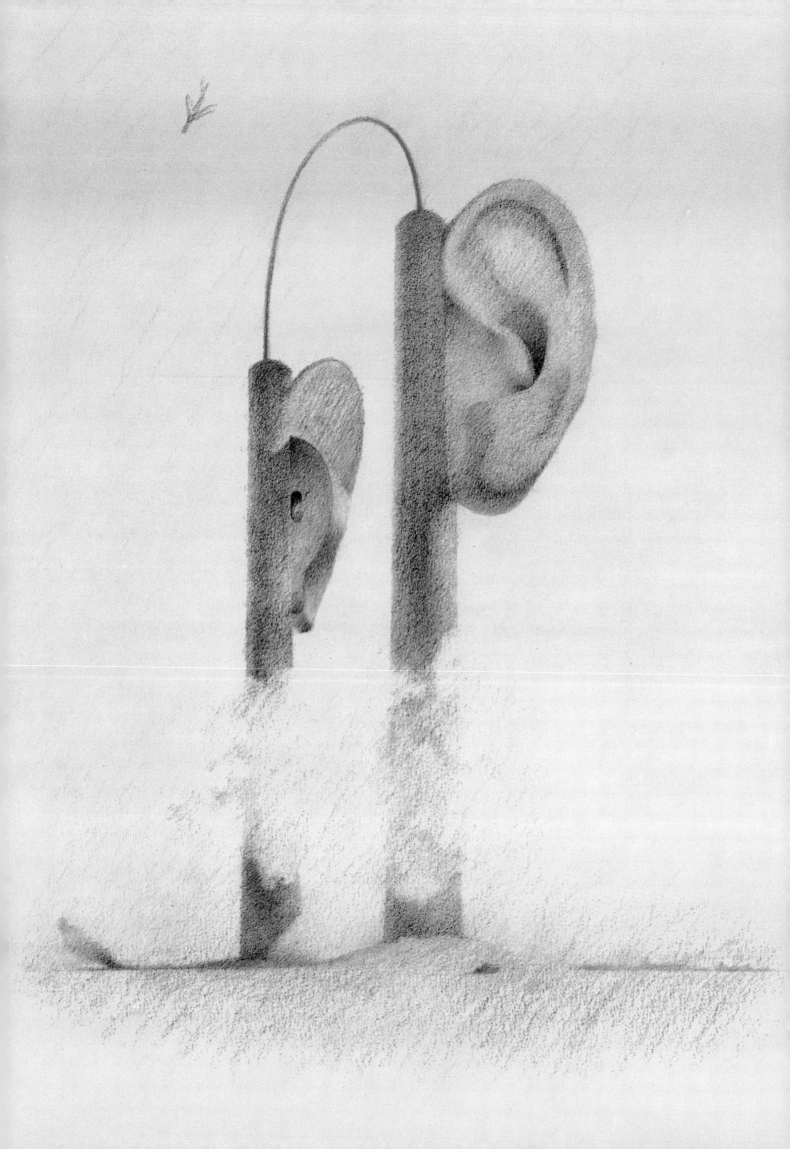

TEXT CONTINUED FROM PAGE 71

such as a bed—as being hard-surfaced instead.

Oldenburg also finds inspiration in whatever he happens to hear. He enjoys hearing stories, like the one somebody in a restaurant once told him about the czar's thumb. Long ago a Russian czar rejected a plan for a new road from Moscow to Leningrad because the prospective route was not straight. Seizing a pencil, the czar tried to draw a straight line between the two cities on the map, but the thumb of his other hand got in the way, so that the resulting line included an arc around the thumb tip. The road was built perfectly straight—except for the half circle around the thumb tip. The towering thumb that Oldenburg proposes as one of the Seven New Wonders of the World (see page 76) was based on this old tale. While working on the Seven New Wonders of the World for HORIZON, he tried sketching the thumb in various positions, but it took the inspiration of a bowl of hot and sour soup in a Chinese restaurant to produce a thumb in what looks to the artist like the right position. He sat at supper, drawing and jabbing his thumb down beside his soup bowl, until he got the effect he wanted.

Pointing to the drawings in his office of such unfeasible plans as an ice-cream-cone derrick or toilet floats bobbing in the Thames, he says, "Everything here is based on my having ideas. So I go to my files, where all my notes and sketches are stored chronologically, to stimulate myself." They are all there, all the way back to Neubern. Not only do the notes inspire finished works, but they themselves were published in facsimile last year in *Notes in Hand: Miniatures of My Notebook Pages.* While the massive files of notes languish, year after year, "waiting for a reason to be drawn," Oldenburg himself moves busily and smoothly in and out of many different roles: lecturer, architect, lionized artist, engineer, lithographer, and tourist. Last year alone, his work took him to Des Moines, Vancouver, Stuttgart, Lon-

don, Osaka, Boston, Oslo, and Pasadena—among other cities. Oldenburg lost forty pounds on his travels, and claims that he swells up or thins down according to the work at hand—a thin Oldenburg for skinny works, a fat Oldenburg for plump ones.

As a connoisseur of all states of opposition, personal or public, Oldenburg is highly sensitive to the clash between men and objects. "My auto is a hypochondriac," he says. "It lies to me, telling me its manifold, or whatever it can think up, is out of order. I kick it, I say: Run, drive, or whatever you call what you do. I can't believe so many parts and details have no sensation."

Obsessed with this contentious relationship with objects, Oldenburg would like to replace our conventional monuments, like the Washington obelisk, with what he calls his "obstacle monuments." "It's an old idea, that a huge monument, like the Arc de Triomphe, should intentionally get in the way, and screw up traffic." His proposal for a monument to Adlai Stevenson consists of a hat fallen upon the pavement; cast in bronze, it could be tripped over —"it represents the way you might feel about Stevenson," Oldenburg says mysteriously. Is it that Stevenson's spirit is a blocking, bothersome one? His war monument would be a 500,-000,000-pound block of concrete to be placed at Broadway and Canal—supposedly the optimum nuclear target in Manhattan—completely blocking that intersection.

Only two of Oldenburg's large monuments have ever been built. The first of these was in New Haven, and the project was sparked by Herbert Marcuse's comment on a Good Humor bar Oldenburg had projected as a replacement for the Pan-Am Building on East 45th Street in New York. Marcuse said that if the Good Humor bar ever went up, "I would say this society has come to an end. Because then people cannot take anything seriously: neither their president, nor the cabinet, nor the corporation executives. . . .

This kind of satire can indeed kill. I think it would be one of the most bloodless means to achieve a radical change." Students at Yale were fascinated by the idea that a *real* Oldenburg monument could bring about a revolution, and they formed a company, the Colossal Keepsake Corporation, to commission Oldenburg to build the "first monument to the second American Revolution." Oldenburg made a twenty-four-foot-high lipstick sitting on tractor treads—an appropriate combination of phallic, warlike, and feminine elements. It made a fine obstacle in the middle of the Yale campus, and remained there more than a year before being vandalized.

The only other big work that Oldenburg has managed to have built was an inflatable ice bag for the U.S. Pavilion at the World's Fair in Japan. Equipped with blowers, it inflated to its full, shivering height and then subsided for a "resting period." Oldenburg built it in a Hollywood factory that specializes in fabricating automated characters for motion pictures. Visiting Japan later, Oldenburg was surprised to find that the Japanese spectators had no idea of what an ice bag was supposed to be for. "It turned out that the ice bag was *really* an exotic object over there," he says cheerfully.

Oldenburg dreams of a world in which major expenditures would be for art, a civilization that could actually build his Seven New Wonders of the World. He believes that his Wonders are akin to the originals because all are beyond belief; the Seven Ancient Wonders are gone except for the Pyramids and a few fragments. As for the social utility of the new ones, each would include observation towers or restaurants where people could take the kids on a Sunday. He loves the idea of people sending home postcards from his Alcatraz foot or his Russian thumb.

Roy Bongartz once wrote a book of interrelated stories called Twelve Chases on West Ninety-Ninth Street—*which may explain why he lives in Rhode Island.*

The World of Saint-Simon

The Duc de Saint-Simon

In his insultingly tiny Versailles room
a noble diarist recorded life
in the court of the Sun King. Prudery, malice,
and considerations of status
filled his pages and produced a masterpiece

By J. H. PLUMB

*Elaborately dressed courtiers stroll past nude statues of the ancients that line the
Galerie des Antiques, one of the formal promenades set in the garden of Versailles.*

To sit or not to sit; to doff one's hat or keep it on. Will one, or will one not, be able to retain the right of sprinkling a royal coffin with holy water? Who shall, and who shall not, hold the king's shirt or pour water over the royal hands or remove the royal dung? Stiff-necked, dressed in clothes as bright as a peacock's feathers, the courtiers of Louis XIV moved about Versailles to the strains of Lully and Couperin like great heraldic beasts caught up in a ritual dance—elegant, stylized, yet intensely taut. Beneath the great wigs, every beady eye would be watching. Was the head inclined so slightly that the courtesy implied insult; was the bow so deep that it hinted at a grovel, so perfectly attuned as to imply friendship based on equal status? A correct assessment might lead to intrigue, power, or disgrace. No world has ever been so formal as Saint-Simon's nor so fearful of hidden danger.

The court of Louis XIV functioned like some elaborate clock, from the hour when the king was dressed in public, to the daily mass in the royal chapel, to the formalized meals and the royal parades when the king and his family passed slowly down the long lines of courtiers, speaking to some, nodding to others—ignoring a few. Daily presence at these rituals was essential. Every tongue would be wagging; the whole atmosphere would be charged with an intensity of emotion that we find hard to appreciate. Unless we do, the world of Saint-Simon will remain closed to us—a boring parade of bewigged nonentities, long dead and, except for the king and a few of his marshals, long forgotten. If we realize that these arts, which Saint-Simon described so passionately and watched so meticulously, were the keys to power, the visible signs of status in a struggle as vivid, as cruel, and at times as final as the mating rituals of stick insects, then the gyrations of these gilded creatures become utterly absorbing.

It is only because day after day, year after year, the Duc de Saint-Simon scribbled down all he saw and heard that it is possible for us to enter fully into the emotions and conflicts that swept through the foul, stinking corridors of Versailles—as vivid in the stench of human flesh and excrement as they were in the dazzlement of courtly costumes. Only a hard, tough, blinkered egotist could have gone on for so long recording the complex, corrupt, power-and-sex-ridden court life of France. But Saint-Simon was such an egotist and he was an obsessed egotist: his privileges as a Duc de France were as dear to him as life itself. Every gesture of the king and his family, every assumption of rights, every breach of protocol, was charged with emotion for him; he would reel off pages on the iniquity of an ambassador's daughter who offered her cheek to be kissed by a princess of the blood. A part of Saint-Simon's magic lies in the way that he makes us feel the passionate horror associated with the breaches of protocol in a hierarchic society that at first sight seems so alien.

It comes as a shock to learn what a wonderful instrument etiquette could be for conveying malice and envy, as well as gratitude, and how skillfully the courtiers of Louis XIV played on it. Gradually, these dukes and marquises, cardinals and countesses, cavorting in their complex dances, take on the lineaments of humanity. Saint-Simon was alive to every nuance, rushing back to his room (an insultingly small one, he felt, but the only one he could get) to set down everything that he had seen and heard.

The result of Saint-Simon's obsession is quite incredible. The full edition of his memoirs runs to forty-three fat volumes, a ziggurat of letters that dominates the history of France during the late seventeenth and early eighteenth centuries. One may hate it or love it, but, just as Saint-Simon would have wanted, no one can ignore it. Although his memoirs certainly helped to assuage his obsessive passions about privilege, Saint-Simon always designed

them to be far more than that. His intention from the first moment he set pen to paper was to be a great historian, to rival the famous Froissart, whose pages had brought alive the France of the Hundred Years' War. He wanted to depict his world. He did.

Louis de Rouvroy was born at Versailles on January 15, 1675. His father, the Duc de Saint-Simon, was sixty-nine years old, and Louis succeeded to the title at the age of eighteen. His education was supervised by his young mother, who was strict and devout. She hated the corruptions of court life, yet she was as concerned with its hierarchic conventions as her son learned to be—only fitting, perhaps, for the Saint-Simons had been elevated to their dukedom quite recently by Louis XIII (whom Saint-Simon of course revered) and, indeed, had at least one bourgeois skeleton in their cupboard (Saint-Simon's grandmother). Saint-Simon had the slapdash education usual for his class: very little academic work, but immense labors at horse-

THE SUN KING

Louis XIV, shown opposite in his coronation robes, was Versailles's undisputed prime mover. "The entire court and everyone else," as Saint-Simon explained to a novice, "suited their behavior to that of the monarch, watching for him to give them the lead." About Louis himself, however, Saint-Simon never quite made up his mind. He recognized the exquisite politeness of the king, "outwardly so equable, so perfectly controlled in his slightest gestures." Yet he considered Louis a totally selfish person, who "had no interest in anyone except himself, and had no regard for anyone else's feelings except his own." As evidence, Saint-Simon noted, for example, what a trial the king's love of fresh air was to Mme de Maintenon, his public mistress and secret wife, for "the poor woman suffered acutely from draughts, which made no difference to Louis XIV. Winter and summer he threw the windows wide open." In truth, the king's power magnified the consequences of every flaw. Once, in a rare display of anger, he struck a footman who had stolen a biscuit, and the whole court, said Saint-Simon, was "frightened to death."

"RIBANDS EVERYWHERE, DRENCHED IN PERFUME"

Philippe, Duc d'Orléans, the king's brother (left), "a little man with a big stomach trotting on high heels," was the kind of high-born ninny around whom upstarts spun their schemes, much to Saint-Simon's chagrin. "There never was a man so flabby in mind and body, so feeble, so timid, so often deceived and so easily led." The fatal weakness of "Monsieur"—his court title—was a passion for handsome boys. Those who won his favor made their fortunes, for, according to the diarist, "they could get anything out of him and in return often treated him with the greatest insolence." A mincing, bedizened chatterbox, "ribands everywhere, drenched in perfume," Monsieur was once exploited even by his own brother. Keen to elevate his "royal bastards," Louis hoped to marry off one of his illegitimate daughters to Monsieur's son, a prince of the royal blood. Since "Monsieur was very sensitive about anything touching his own position," Louis called for the services of the handsome Chevalier de Lorraine, who, according to Saint-Simon, had "established a lifelong ascendency" over Monsieur. Quickly caving in, the king's brother glumly approved the unseemly betrothal. For services rendered, the chevalier demanded a Knighthood of the Order of the Holy Spirit. And the reward was to be "paid in advance," noted Saint-Simon, who was never one to overlook a nuance.

manship, swordsmanship, dancing, and military exercises. He developed quite early in life, however, an insatiable appetite for history. "This reading of history," he later wrote, "especially private memoirs of my own period and that immediately after the reign of François I, gave me the idea of writing down my own observations, in the hope that by learning all I could of current affairs I might eventually fit myself for some high office."

At twenty he went off to fight in Louis XIV's endless wars against the Dutch; he took his pen as well as his sword and employed the former far more frequently. For the next thirty years or so, with few intermissions, Saint-Simon lived at court, usually, however, on its fringes, for Louis XIV had no high opinion of his merits and rather disliked him "for being very heated on matters concerning precedent," as Saint-Simon himself admitted. Yet he was always close enough to witness and record the tragedy of Louis XIV's declining years. He was closer still to the farcical and macabre Regency of the Duc d'Orléans that followed the king's death.

The center of Saint-Simon's world was the king, whom he watched with reverence and loathing. Louis XIV was a tiny man of vast dignity, an insatiable sexual appetite that hardly diminished, even in advanced old age, and a capacity for work commensurate with his potency. After a desperate childhood and adolescence, during which France was racked with aristocratic civil wars that reduced the monarchy to penury, he had built up the power and glory of France to Augustan proportions: indeed, Augustan Rome was Louis's ideal, and an ideal achieved. By 1689 France dominated western Europe not only politically but culturally as well, particularly in the literary and decorative arts. The European aristocracy flocked to Versailles to learn how to live and to bask momentarily in the reflected rays of Louis's greatness. He took the sun for his symbol—the center of radiance, the giver of life, the promoter of growth. And, though he lived in great luxury and extravagance, Louis always put France first.

Saint-Simon, however, hated him; hated particularly the way that he pro-

moted men of bourgeois origins, men like Colbert, the great finance minister who had done so much to extend the commerce and add to the riches of France. Saint-Simon, prudish and conventional, also deplored Louis's sexual appetites, his mistresses and their bastards, whom Louis loved as much as his legitimate children. Above all, Saint-Simon loathed Mme de Maintenon, Louis's morganatic wife. Saint-Simon sneered at her as the "Widow Scarron" because she had been married previously to the playwright Paul Scarron and had at one time been a governess to Louis's bastard children. To Saint-Simon she was "born in the gutter and a disgrace to the royal bed." No disdain was too great for her. Her discretion, piety, modesty, and reticence meant nothing. She came from the wrong womb, and that was final.

*B*ut Louis XIV failed Saint-Simon in minor as well as major matters. He depicts the king as a man without love, cold, cowardly, inhuman. And he never tires of anecdotes that illustrate the king's failings—anecdotes, however, that often enough illus-

Charlotte-Elizabeth, Duchesse d'Orléans (right), was the opposite of her husband in almost every way. Whereas the effeminate Monsieur loved baubles, boys, and social amusements, Madame —a princess of the Palatinate—preferred horses, letter writing, and solitude. According to Saint-Simon, she "spent her days in a study . . . gazing at portraits of German Princes with which the walls were hung, and writing volumes of letters all day and every day." Blunt-spoken and bigoted, "full of likes and dislikes," Madame "made herself feared by her ferocious ill-humor and her tart remarks." Although Monsieur "lived on quite good terms with her," said the diarist, "he almost never saw her alone." When Louis affianced his illegitimate daughter to her son, Madame, who was "inexorable on the matter of propriety," wept with impotent fury in full view of the king and the court. To a "princess of the old stamp," as Saint-Simon described her, such a *mésalliance* was a mortifying blow, and "when her son approached her to kiss her hand" the day after the betrothal was announced, "she smacked his face so hard that the sound of it echoed in the presence of the whole court." Loyal, sullen, and disagreeable, "ignoring all contrivances and niceties," Madame was extremely ill-suited to the court life of Versailles. "Very German in her ways," summed up Saint-Simon.

trate nothing more than Saint-Simon's malice, for many of these tales have been proved to be quite false. When old servants died, Louis XIV expressed no emotion, it is true, and in battle he was circumspect. But the reason for this was that Louis understood the ritual arts of kingship. Kings did not weep in public, nor did they get killed in battle. "I am the state," Louis said, and he meant it. He behaved as if he were. Even on his deathbed, dying inch by inch of gangrene, he showed the same strict dignity that only powerful self-control could sustain. Kings died, as they lived, in public, symbols of greatness. And the same ideal of kingship was responsible for the act that enraged Saint-Simon most: in 1714 Louis gave the royal bastards the right of royal succession. This is the great horror story of the memoirs.

Like a figure of ancient tragedy, Louis XIV in his old age suffered the hammer blows of fate. His country staggered to defeat in the War of the Spanish Succession. Blenheim, Malplaquet, Ramillies, Oudenarde—these victories of the great Duke of Marlborough drained France's armies and her

finances; harvests failed and famine was widespread; the curse of God seemed to be on the land. When Louis's son, his grandson the Duke of Burgundy, and his grandson's wife followed each other to the grave within a year, accompanied by *their* eldest son, Louis's great-grandson, aged five—alive one day, black with fever the next—the king decided he was being punished for his sins, for the riotous sexuality of his youth, with the lovely La Vallière and lovelier Montespan. His sole heir was a puny great-grandson, not yet weaned.

But the state must survive, and could only do so, Louis felt, through the king's own children; otherwise, the aristocrats would be at each other's throats again, as they had been during his youth. So Louis insisted on giving the rank of prince of the blood to all his grown-up bastard sons. Saint-Simon, blind to the state's necessities, could see it merely as an intrigue of the wretched "Widow Scarron." He could not see that, as always, when the state was in conflict with the heraldic world, Louis XIV put the state first. But after the king's death in 1715, the sickly baby survived and became Louis XV; the

king's legitimate nephew, the Duc d'Orléans, became regent, and the bastards, much to Saint-Simon's joy, were denied the right of succession.

And yet, though he hated him, Saint-Simon could not suppress a sense of reverence, almost of admiration, as Louis XIV moved with dignity through his court. One comes to understand why Louis dominated his age as well as his court and country. Saint-Simon might swallow lies and derogatory stories about his king, but he is such an artist, such a quick-eyed witness, that the greatness of Louis shines through.

Indeed, Saint-Simon's greatest quality lies in his ability to depict human beings in all their diversity and to give us a sense of the strange necessities that impelled them. He re-creates an enclosed and narrow world, and depicts the people within it with such care that we know them almost as well as we know ourselves, and recognize our common humanity. This is a great tour de force, for Louis XIV and his courtiers lived in a most exotic atmosphere. The world of court life acted like a

"THE ANCIENT WHORE"

Françoise, Marquise de Maintenon (left) entered the court as the nurse of Louis's illegitimate children, secretly became his wife, c. 1683, and filled Saint-Simon's caste-ridden heart with loathing. "The sewers from which she sprang," was the way he described her background, although Mme de Maintenon was the widow of a celebrated writer. "The ancient whore," he called her in 1715—she was eighty at the time—although she was, in truth, a sort of quintessential governess: decent, respectable, fundamentally dowdy. The king's "habit of deferring" to her judgment of people gave Mme de Maintenon enormous influence at court, but she was easily taken in by affectations of piety, a source of malicious glee to Saint-Simon. According to the diarist, when a young court debauchee, the son of one of her favorites, fell ill he completely hoodwinked his doting mother and the equally doting Maintenon with his professions of religious fervor. Mme de Maintenon went about citing the rascal as a model of virtue, which, said the diarist, "provided a spectacle that diverted the entire court and make a mockery of Mme de Maintenon." Her fundamental decency, however, even Saint-Simon admitted on occasion. When a defeated general lost the king's favor and was shunned by all, "Mme de Maintenon was sorry for him; occasionally she received him and this small honor," said Saint-Simon, "kept him from total extinction."

hothouse, forcing human character into strange extravagances. These French aristocrats, even the humblest of them, felt themselves to be demigods, and they usually behaved as they wished, obeying only the rituals of the court. Ambition, pride, jealousy, and malice ruled the court. Saint-Simon tells the story of an evening's amusement at the expense of a ducal cuckold:

"M de Luxembourg was probably the only person in France who had no idea of what his wife was up to: she was so nice to him that he never suspected her. . . . M. de Luxembourg was very friendly with Monsieur le Duc, M. le Prince de Conti, and Monsieur le Prince [the Prince de Condé, premier prince of the blood royal], and there was no doubt that the last-named was the leading authority on anything to do with parties . . . and so M. de Luxembourg went to him for advice as to what he should wear. Monsieur le Prince, who was as malicious as any man who ever lived and who never felt warmly towards anyone, promised that he would do so—seeing a good chance

to have some fun himself and amuse the whole court; he said that M. de Luxembourg should have supper with him and afterwards he would dress him suitably for the ball.

"These balls at Marly, whether formal or masked, were the same as those at Versailles with the dancers drawn up in two lines—at one end there was a chair for the King, or three if the King and Queen of England were going to be present, as they often were. And on either side the royal family was assembled in a straight line. . . . Sometimes in the middle of the ball Mme la Duchesse and Mme la Princesse de Conti would move in, pretending they were talking to someone, and tack themselves on to the end of the line. . . . When it was a masked ball everyone formed up with his face uncovered and his mask in his hand; but sometime after the ball had begun there were new arrivals, and some of those who had been there already went out to change their clothes, so that when they came back masked, no one knew who was who.

"I had just arrived at the ball and sat down when I saw in front of me a figure draped in some sort of muslin,

light and floating, surmounted by a fantastic headdress including a pair of enormous stag's horns which went up so high that they got caught in one of the chandeliers. Everyone wondered who it could be, and then when he turned around and we saw that it was M. de Luxembourg there was an absolutely outrageous burst of laughter. A few minutes later he came and sat down between the Comte de Toulouse and myself, and the Count asked what had put the idea for such a costume into his head—but the victim was not sharp enough to detect the edge in the question: in fact he was not very bright altogether, and looked about him benignly, regarding the raucous laughter as a tribute to the originality of his get-up. He told all and sundry that he had supped with Monsieur le Prince, who had designed his costume for him, and he bowed to right and left so that his headdress could the better be admired. Then the ladies entered, and immediately after them the King. There was renewed laughter, and M. de Luxembourg went the rounds presenting himself to the company with a ravishing self-assurance. His wife, although she

Marie-Adélaïde, Duchesse de Bourgogne (right) was Versailles's most radiant figure—"the life and light of the court," said Saint-Simon, from the day she arrived in 1696 as the eleven-year-old fiancée of the king's eldest grandson. "Her dazzling situation," as the diarist termed it, was due in part to the court's expectation that she would one day be queen, and in far greater part to the love she inspired in the aged king and Mme de Maintenon. Carefree and merry, she "caressed them, made them laugh . . . tried continually to please them, and treated them with a familiarity which they found enchanting." Except for a plain face, the little duchess was remarkably like a fairy-tale princess. Graceful of figure, with a "small but admirable bust," as Saint-Simon noted, she "walked like a goddess on the clouds," flitting "hither and thither like a nymph." "She was so kind," said Saint-Simon, "that she dreaded causing the least pain to anyone," and so "unaffected" that she "lived on terms of easy intimacy" with everyone. The whole court "lived to please her," and what pleased the young duchess were parties, balls, dancing, and madcap jests. One season she invited Saint-Simon to attend all her parties, and as a result of this, said the diarist, "I did not see the light of day for three weeks." When she died at the age of twenty-seven, even the self-centered Saint-Simon was deeply moved. "All joy vanished . . . and darkness covered the court."

knew quite well that her way of life was common knowledge, blushed deeply; and the whole court laughed at the pair of them. . . ."

If malice was rife, so were sexuality in all its forms, exhibitionism, drunkenness, gourmandising, and every other vice. "Everything in excess" might have been the court's motto, whether it be piety in Mme de Maintenon or the endless letter writing—millions of words a year—of the fat German sister-in-law of Louis XIV, Liselotte, whose correspondence is almost as fascinating as Saint-Simon's memoirs.

We can witness through Saint-Simon's pages the corroding effects of privilege. And he never evades the blemishes. He adored the Duke of Burgundy, the grandson who died in 1712, for the duke was as obsessed with protocol as Saint-Simon was himself. Although Saint-Simon could write of him in terms that bordered on blasphemy ("What a clear reflection of the Divinity appeared in his pure soul, so strong, so simple, retaining in as high a degree as is permitted here below the image of its Creator")

and go on to liken him to Christ on the Cross, he could not disguise the truth. He does not deny the duke's fabulous temper, "subject to transports of rage even against inanimate objects"; nor does he gloss the fact that he was "mad for all kinds of amusement, a woman-lover and at the same time, which is rare, with an equally strong propensity in another direction."

If Saint-Simon could not bring himself to hide the failings of his hero, his enemies naturally got short shrift. And what a welter of unsavory habits they had! Homosexuality, adultery, occasional incest, exploitation of children, wife-swapping, priapism, pornography —every form of sexual diversion flourished at Louis's court and at that of the regent who followed him. The first truly permissive societies were the aristocratic courts of Europe; what the masses are beginning to practice was formerly the privilege of the few. California has only just begun to catch up with eighteenth-century Versailles.

Still, Versailles was more than a place to misbehave in; it had its public face as well. It was the hub of government: ministers and ambassadors lived

there among the courtiers, and Saint-Simon observed Louis XIV's government as well as his private life.

For most of his reign Louis XIV was at war. Seventeenth-century Europe witnessed an increase in government activity—more armies and navies to mobilize and conduct, strategy and treaties to debate, foreign relations to manipulate. All final decisions rested with the king at Versailles, and every day Louis worked away for hours at his desk, like any clerk. Throughout Saint-Simon's volumes is heard the rumble of guns, the storm of battle, and although he was more concerned with the conflicts between generals or their relations with Louis, he does make us aware of the extreme difficulties that faced France, indeed, faced all governments at that time. The greatest problem was to raise armies and mobilize navies. To provision them, equip them, and lead them were superhuman tasks simply because methods of organization were so primitive. The farther one got from Versailles, the weaker the king's authority. Outside the court Louis XIV's supposedly absolute power was limited. He could

André Le Nôtre, Versailles's great gardener, had a "naiveté and straightforwardness," said Saint-Simon, "which charmed everyone," including the king, who enjoyed his blunt speech. A formalist, Le Nôtre used to say, reported Saint-Simon, "the flower beds at Versailles were of no use to anyone except nurses who could not leave the children in their charge and needed something to look at out of the second-floor windows."

Hyacinthe Rigaud, self-portrayed above, was the chief painter at court, "the best in Europe for catching likenesses," according to Saint-Simon. Determined to have him portray his spiritual adviser, an austere Trappist monk, Saint-Simon introduced the painter to the monk in the guise of a fellow army officer. Rigaud stared at the old man's face for nearly an hour, then rushed home to paint his portrait from memory.

Jean Baptiste Racine, "so celebrated for his magnificent plays," said Saint-Simon, "was friends with the highest ranking members of the court," where he served as Louis's royal biographer. He also wrote two plays for St. Cyr, a school founded by Mme de Maintenon. Racine "did not act the poet," said Saint-Simon, paying him a high compliment, "but was . . . decent, modest, and, towards the end, a perfect gentleman."

promote or dismiss generals; he could (and did) attend a siege of a fortress—one of the great set pieces of seventeenth-century warfare—but he could not stem the tide of incompetence and corruption that ebbed and flowed about his armies.

Records, methods of accounting, trained clerks—they did not exist. The authority of any modern government, even the most feeble state in Africa, is far greater than Louis XIV's, simply because it can impose its will at any given time on most of its subjects. Louis XIV could not. His power over individuals, over immediate events and decisions, was great, but also transient, depending on his presence or on the presence of dedicated royal officials, and these were in all too short supply. Saint-Simon vividly describes how the king himself was disillusioned with Maréchal Villars, one of his generals:

"Villars had been reappointed to Flanders, but viewed his task with great disfavor. Having risen to unparalleled heights of favor, privilege, wealth, and rank, he believed that for the first time in his life he might safely deliver a few unpalatable truths [concerning the wretched state of Louis's officers and men, and their lack of ammunition and supplies] . . . He ventured to state his complaints quite baldly to the King and Mme de Maintenon. . . . The scene which he revealed appeared to them so terrible, so monstrously shocking, that they found it easier to be angry than accept such language from Villars, who had always been their comforter . . . Now that he voiced the unanimous opinion of all the rest of the army, their faith in him was shattered along with his power to delude them in the hope of personal advantage. They saw him for the first time as he seemed to the world in general, absurd, crazy, impudent, lying, wholly irresponsible."

*U*nless we understand the king's weakness, Saint-Simon's world will be mysterious. We cannot comprehend the fear and uncertainty that threaded through the lives of the great. So long as Louis was alive, so was his vast personal authority, but the machine he manipulated was inefficient. Political life was personal to a degree we find difficult to grasp, emotionally if not intellectually. Saint-Simon, however, helps us grasp it.

As soon as Louis died, the forces of instability were unleashed: no one's head, let alone his office or salary, was safe. With the majestic authority of the king gone, the machinery of government was too weak, the idea of the state too feeble, to check the personal jealousies of his survivors or control their lust for power. Fortunately for France, Louis had so built up the concept of regal authority, so neatly clipped the wings of the aristocracy, so strengthened the feeble sinews of government, that the throne survived. The possibility of *coup d'état*, of factional triumph at court and the redistribution of power that would follow, gave even the most influential at court a sense of living on a razor's edge.

One has only to think of Mme de Maintenon's last days at court. Louis's death stripped her not only of power but of social status. One day she was the most powerful woman in France, the next the obscure guest of a convent. In Saint-Simon's world such whirligigs of fate were a part of life, breeding fear and perhaps driving men and women to-

Jacques Bossuet, Bishop of Meaux and tutor to Louis's heir apparent, was France's most formidable defender of established dogmas. He had considerable entrée with the king, said Saint-Simon, and had "on many occasions been the sole witness of the angry scenes" between Louis and Mme de Montespan, Louis's early mistress. This far from pleasant privilege created a lifetime bond between the bishop and the king.

Jean Baptiste Lully founded the French school of opera while serving as master of music for the royal family at Versailles. The post, which Lully held until his death in 1687, was a busy one, since Louis loved music and wanted it played constantly. Lully not only composed the music, he managed the orchestras, ensembles, and festivities that were constantly requested by courtiers ever anxious to emulate the king.

Michel Richard de Lalande, master of the royal chapel from 1704 to 1726, was the second notable composer, after Lully, to preside over the musical establishment of Versailles. By Lalande's time, the king had lost his early taste for Lully's crashing brasses, but not his fondness for music. Whenever Lalande was composing a piece for him, he would summon the musician several times a day to discuss its progress.

ward a world of immediate sensation in which the future was drowned. That is why the deaths of Louis's heirs and of Louis himself form the climax of Saint-Simon's memoirs, for not only did his own future hang in the balance (he was a great friend of the young dauphin who died before Louis), but so did the careers of half the court of France.

It was this sense of the instability of life that had haunted Louis himself—the greatest character, to my mind, in the memoirs. At first sight Louis seems paradoxical: massively hard-working, endlessly toiling with his ministers and yet never missing the solemn ritualistic acts that punctuated his days—the formal dressing and undressing, the public meals, the regular hunts and balls and drawing rooms. And yet, as one reads book after book of the memoirs, one comes to see that this life style of Louis was as deliberate as his creation of Versailles or his foundation of the Académie Française. Louis's father, Louis XIII, and grandfather, Henry IV, and he himself had each lived through civil wars fomented by rebellious aristocrats. By skill at home and victory abroad Louis had tied the aristocracy

to his apron strings, but the strings could easily snap, and so Louis heightened the image of kingship to create a special regal world—far richer, more luxurious, and more powerful than any individual could obtain for himself. By thus elevating the monarchy, Louis hoped not only to increase its power but also to breed respect and awe, so that opposition to the royal will would savor of sacrilege, and be inhibited. To achieve this end, Louis XIV wanted not only semi-mystical rituals but also a theatre in which Divine Kingship could be enacted.

*H*ence Versailles. Saint-Simon had been born there, and it remained the center of his universe; and when, in 1724, he lost his place at court, his memoirs stopped; for his last thirty years he lived so obscurely that we know little about him. Without Versailles, life was without interest, and this was true not only for Saint-Simon but also for most of the nobility of France. That was exactly Louis's intention. This monstrous palace, still the greatest in Europe, the largest built since the fall of the Roman

Empire, was the wonder of its day. The vast reception room—the *Galerie des Glaces*—was a triumph of seventeenth-century technology as well as of the decorative arts, for its windows and mirrors were made possible only by the new techniques of French glassmaking. In the rooms the richness of France was displayed in tapestries, furniture, carpets, and the splendid portraits by Rigaud. The palace roof covered literally acres of rooms—enough to house the government, the foreign embassies, the personal court of the king, his brother, and their children, their mistresses, their bastards, and the hundreds of aristocrats who were given the special blue cloak that indicated their right to free rooms and free food. Outside the palace there were miles of parterres, scores of fountains, beyond anything previously known to the seventeenth century; a huge orangery; walks and riding paths that gradually dissolved into miles of forest, where the court hunted.

Everything was larger than life, deliberately so; for Louis XIV meant to proclaim not only his own strength but also the grandeur of France and the

THE GENERAL AND HIS CHAISE-PERCÉE

Louis, Duc de Vendôme (left), the best French general of his day, was a dissolute aristocrat who loved to outrage his fellow noblemen, Saint-Simon included. The grandson of a French king, Vendôme once informed the court he was leaving Versailles for a syphilis cure—the disease ate away most of his nose—thus becoming, said Saint-Simon, "the first person who ever dared formally to take his leave of the King for the purpose." Gluttonous and lazy, Vendôme not only practiced "unnatural vice," he was "quite open about it," and surrounded himself with serv-

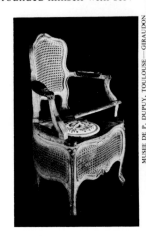

ants and junior officers who "satisfied his perverted tastes." Cleanliness he deemed mere affectation. In the field each morning he would make distinguished visitors attend him while he sat on his *chaise-percée*, a chamber pot embedded in a chair, much like that at right. "Still sitting there," said Saint-Simon, "he would then eat an enormous breakfast with two or three friends ... According to him, these were simple habits, without frills, worthy of the ancient Romans."

impotence of nobility. Heraldic beasts the aristocrats might be, but they were caged. Versailles, the army, occasionally diplomacy—these careers were open to them as long as the king regarded them with favor. Otherwise, they faced exile in the provinces—dullness and disgrace. This is the fear that runs through Saint-Simon's memoirs and spreads terror as soon as it looms into reality.

Versailles, of course, was not by our standards all beauty and grace. There were no bathrooms, and the stench of the stairways, where courtiers frequently relieved themselves, was appalling. Saint-Simon refers to the odor of a royal person and the foulness of his breath as the most natural things in the world, and indeed they were. This lack of hygiene introduced into Saint-Simon's world a character as alarming as the king himself—Death. Typhoid, scarlet fever, puerperal fever, putrid fever, yellow fever, and diptheria skidded around the corridors of Versailles, knocking out a prince of the blood here or an obscure courtier there. The pattern of power could change overnight, bringing hope or disaster to the court.

And this, too, added to the hothouse atmosphere, driving people to an extravagance of license or piety. Death, corruption, disease—these were but the shadows in that brilliant gilded world that was to set a pattern for monarchs and their courts for a hundred years.

At a time when aristocratic power was on the resurgent in Europe, Louis created a standard of monarchic and aristocratic elegance that all lesser kings envied and attempted to emulate, so that to understand this world through Saint-Simon's eyes helps us understand the courts of eighteenth-century Europe, such as Frederick the Great's at San Souci or the king of Naples's at Caserta. Like Louis, they poured millions into building their palaces and adorning them with all the arts and crafts that adorn the life of man. But Louis did more than that.

Versailles contains a great theatre, and those vast galleries were made for music. Louis, especially as a young man in the 1670's and 1680's, drew to his court a galaxy of talent. His courtiers could see some of the greatest plays ever written in the French language—some, like the tragedies of Corneille, dated from a previous generation, others, like Racine's masterpieces, belonged to their own time. And Versailles also provided a stage for Molière, the greatest comic dramatist France has ever known. Louis could be remarkably tolerant; after all, he enjoyed the fables of La Fontaine, which were often sharply critical of grandeur and cynical about worldly success. As with literature, so with music: Lully, Couperin, and Rameau wrote the dances and ballets and early operas that brought France's music to a height rivaling that of Italy. The music, like the plays of Molière or the fables of La Fontaine, seems at first hearing to be delicate and superficial, yet the attentive ear can discern a deeper note, a sense of life's transience, a knowledge that everything ends in darkness. Such music is peculiarly appropriate for the gilded world of Versailles—elegant and brittle, yet intensely human. And, as Louis XIV intended, it came to be regarded as the finest in Europe, and it advertised the Sun King in all his splendor.

Of course, it was a private world; in

Of all the monstrous figures who flourished at Versailles none was more like a creature of melodrama than the Princesse d'Harcourt, a fearsome witch whose "character," said Saint-Simon, "throws light on the nature of the court at which she was received." In her youth a beauty and "very free with her favors," the princess had become in middle age "a big fat creature, always in a bustle, with a muddy complexion, thick ugly lips and tow-colored hair which was always coming undone and untidy like her dirty squalid clothes." A glutton who "gorged herself without scruple," the princess, above all, was "avaricious and greedy," a schemer who "grew rich on the families she had ruined," yet "worked just as hard for a hundred francs as she would for a hundred thousand." Deceitful and shameless, the princess habitually cheated at cards and "made no bones about it. If she was caught, she begged pardon and got away with it; it came to be regarded as a natural hazard of playing at court." Yet far from being denounced, the princess was "dreaded by the whole court, up to the Princesses and even the King's Ministers." The reason for this was quite simple: the court was ruled by favor, and the princess, a devout churchgoer, was a "great favorite of Mme de Maintenon." The rule of favor, however, was a two-edged weapon. To the very few who outranked her, the princess was chiefly a butt of jests. The dauphin and the Duchesse de Bourgogne, for example, "were always perpetrating practical jokes on her," such as setting off firecrackers under her sedan chair. One winter night the duchess led a party into the old harridan's bedroom and pelted her with snowballs for half an hour. Against such pranks as these the princess was helpless, for "in the eyes of the King and Mme de Maintenon the young Duchess could do no wrong." Thanks to her fondness for jests, the court got a measure of vicarious revenge on the princess, "although otherwise," as Saint-Simon said, "it was inadvisable to offend her." At Versailles, only the king himself was truly safe.

a sense, a theatre that the rest of France and Europe watched, for beyond Versailles lay the twenty million Frenchmen who toiled to maintain Louis XIV, his army, and his ambition. They rarely stray across the pages of Saint-Simon. Yet there were times when even he had to take note of their plight. In 1709 famine swept France in the wake of the disastrous war in Spain, and hundreds of thousands died of starvation. Briefly, the blackened faces of the peasants obtruded in Saint-Simon's world and sent a *frisson* of horror down his aristocratic spine. And here lies the key to the deepest tragedy of Louis XIV's world: he created a mirage of aristocratic elegance, grandeur, wit, and indulgence played out against a background of ostentatious art and beauty, but totally divorced from the nation that he led.

An aristocrat's social obligation was to the monarch and to the state, to Louis and Versailles, not to the people and the countryside. This became the pattern of all European aristocracies except the British. The result was the tumbrels, the guillotines, the gallows, and the firing squads, as it is bound to be for any aristocracy that puts self-indulgence and loyalty to its own class and its own ruler before its obligations to society. Civilizations and cultures that ignore the condition of ordinary humanity end in ruin. That is the moral lesson of Saint-Simon, as appropriate to our own day as to his.

The courtiers of Versailles would have thought it in no way wrong to spend five and a half million dollars on a Velázquez while the peasants starved in rat-infested huts. Their private world of privilege and elegance divorced them from the realities of life; and so to read Saint-Simon is not merely to enter into a world alien to our own, although it *is* alien, but also to see ourselves, even in the distorting mirrors of time. Nothing may be the same, but we always remain so. The privileged are always at risk, and they are never more so than when they look fixedly inward to their own world.

Perhaps that is the meaning of Saint-Simon. At first sight his world is strange and remote, limited to a handful of overprivileged aristocrats living in the hothouse atmosphere that forced their personalities into the most exotic shapes. But as we read and brood, this world of envy, malice, ambition, piety, love, and loyalty becomes recognizably our own.

As Louis XIV told him, Saint-Simon undoubtedly talked too much; certainly he wrote too much, but little was missed by that spider who watched from his little web in Versailles, darting out at the least ripple on the glittering surface of the court to seize his victim and wrap him up in the coils of his prose, preserving him for all time. He thus achieved the immortality and the fame that he thought were his by rank. Without his skill, his dedication and stamina, greater even than that of the bourgeois clerks he despised, he would be but a name in a genealogy. A cynical thought that the Duc de Saint-Simon would not have enjoyed.

However, there he is—detestable as a man yet great as an artist. His macabre picture of the court of the aging king of France is as lurid, as melodramatic, as a landscape by Salvator Rosa. This is how a literary artist of genius saw his world. As great art should, it will hold the mind and trouble the heart of anyone who has the patience to study it.

Three generations of Bourbon royalty sur-
round Louis XIV in a portrait by Nicolas
de Largillière. Leaning on the king's chair
is the heir apparent, the dauphin, in a flowing blond periwig. Standing at right is the
dauphin's son and heir, the Duc de Bourgogne, one of whose children is shown with
the governess, the Duchesse de Ventadour.
Louis outlived them all. In 1711 smallpox
killed the characterless dauphin, a man,
said Saint-Simon, "without vice, virtue,
knowledge or understanding . . . capable
only of being bored and affecting others by
his ennui," an heir to the throne whom
Louis was so determined to nullify that,
said Saint-Simon, "if he showed a preference for anyone, it was quite enough to put
paid to that person's hopes forever."

Several months later, a far greater blow
struck the Bourbon dynasty. First, the
Duchesse de Bourgogne, the new dauphine,
fell ill with measles, was profusely bled and
purged by the doctors, and died shortly after, plunging the king into "the only real
grief which he ever experienced." The next
day her husband appeared at the king's
levee with his face, as the diarist observed
in horror, covered with spots. Put to bed,
purged, and bled, he, too, died of measles.
Two weeks later, measles and the medical
men carried off *his* five-year-old son and
heir. "Thus, in less than a year," said
Saint-Simon, "three dauphins had died,"
stunning not only the court but all Europe.

What saved the succession, ironically,
was the widespread belief that poison had
caused the deaths. When measles struck the
newest heir, the infant Duc d'Anjou, "The
Duchesse de Ventadour . . . kidnapped him
and stubbornly refused to let him be bled."
She had an antidote to the "poison," which,
she believed, would not work after blood-
letting. Safely out of the doctor's hands,
the infant "recovered, and is our King today." Louis survived the blows to his
House and family for three more years, but
the sun was fast setting on the court of Versailles. Its heyday was already over, and before the end of the century revolution would
sweep it away. The splendor and squalor,
the intricate gyrations of that glittering little world, would scarcely be imaginable
without the record kept by Saint-Simon: "to
whom nobody pays any attention," as the
Prussian ambassador remarked, not realizing Saint-Simon would have the last word.

Who Got Here First?

Refugees from Atlantis? Phoenicians piloting the children of Israel?
Chinese? Egyptians? Or none of them? A noted authority on early ship
travel dares to think the unthinkable about the discovery of America

By LIONEL CASSON

In 1641 a Portuguese Jew named Antonio Montezinos, while journeying near Quito in Ecuador, met up with a native who, he was flabbergasted to discover, was Jewish. What is more, the man took him on an arduous week-long trip through the hinterland to a remote spot where an entire community of Jews was living; Antonio actually heard them recite in Hebrew the traditional prayer, "Hear, O Israel."

Returning to Europe, he reported this spectacular news to Manasseh ben Israel, the most eminent Jewish scholar of the day. Manasseh published it in a slim volume called *The Hope of Israel,* which was swiftly translated from Spanish into Latin, Hebrew, and English; the English version went into three editions within two years. Manasseh was not the first to claim that the Lost Tribes of Israel had crossed the ocean to America, but he was the one who really launched the notion on its long-lived career.

The theory that wandering Israelites were among the founders of New World civilization reached its heyday

in the last century. Lord Kingsborough of England, for example, went through the family fortune and landed in debtors' prison no less than three times in order to publish deluxe volumes proving that the Mexican Indians were descendants of the Lost Tribes. And the Mormon sacred writings speak of two waves of Israelite migrants, an early wave of Jaredites, who found their way across the Atlantic during the confused times after the toppling of the Tower of Babel and a later one made up of the followers of a certain Lehi, who left Jerusalem about 600 B.C., shortly before the rest of the city was led off into the Babylonian captivity.

How the émigrés negotiated the thousands of miles of open water bothered no one, since the Bible had a built-in explanation. The Lost Tribes had presumably gotten themselves lost sometime after 721 B.C., the year that Sargon II of Assyria conquered the northern part of Palestine and resettled its inhabitants in the upper reaches of the Tigris and Euphrates. At least two

centuries before this, Solomon had "made a navy of ships in Ezion-geber . . . on the shore of the Red Sea," which he manned with Phoenician "shipmen that had knowledge of the sea" and which "came to Ophir, and fetched from thence gold . . . and silver, ivory, and apes, and peacocks." If the ships of the day could make it to Ophir and back—a three years' journey, we are told—obviously they could take an Atlantic crossing in stride.

The Bible pointedly mentions that Solomon used Phoenician crews. The Phoenicians were for a long while the mariners par excellence of the ancient world. They even boasted considerable oceanic expertise: not only did they sail to Ophir but, according to a tale reported by Herodotus, around 600 B.C. a fleet of Phoenician galleys successfully circumnavigated the continent of Africa.

With such impeccable nautical references, it was inevitable that the Phoenicians sooner or later would qualify as early transatlantic voyagers. One of their champions, writing in 1822,

Old World meets New: A landing party from distant places rushes ashore, eager to instruct the American aborigine in the arts of civilization.

claimed that he knew of a manuscript —no longer available for consultation, of course—drawn up by a Phoenician named Votan who had seen the Tower of Babel being built and had come to the New World when forced out of his homeland by the Israelites. A few decades later, someone else "proved" that the Mayas were descended from the inhabitants of Tyre.

And, just four years ago, Cyrus Gordon, a well-known professor of Semitic languages who has a penchant for breathless arrival at controversial conclusions, announced in *The New York Times* his discovery of proof positive that a group of Phoenicians had landed in Brazil. He came on it by the sort of miraculous luck usually reserved for the nonacademics in the field. The chance purchase of a scrapbook for a few pennies at a benefit sale led to the discovery of a letter, written by a nineteenth-century savant, that contained a transcription of a stone inscribed in Phoenician characters; the stone had been found by a slave on a Brazilian plantation in 1872 and had been copied

off by the owner's son. The inscription conveniently supplied all the desired details: the identity of the party that had erected the stone (businessmen from Sidon), the date (nineteenth year of Hiram), the point of departure (Ez-ion-geber, just like Solomon's expeditions to Ophir). The original stone, naturally, had long ago gone the way of Votan's manuscript.

Around the beginning of the nineteenth century the drums started to beat loud and strong for the ancient Egyptians as ocean voyagers. Napoleon's Nile campaign had opened up the country to savants and scholars. The Western world, awed at the sudden revelation of what had been achieved there in the days of the Pharaohs, was ready and eager to accept ancient Egypt as the fountainhead of all civilization. So, when European visitors to Mexico returned with glowing tales of the spectacular monuments reared by the people who had lived there long ago, monuments that were sometimes pyramidal in shape or decorated with hieroglyphic carving, everything seemed to fall into

place: migrants from the Nile must somehow have had a hand in shaping what happened in the New World.

But the claim for the Egyptians raised a nautical problem, and a difficult one. They were a river and valley people, presumably with limited maritime skill; how did they get from the banks of the Nile to the shores of Mexico? An answer was found in Plato's tale about an imaginary continent called Atlantis.

The countless words that have been written about the "lost Atlantis" all go back to a handful of pages in the dialogues the *Timaeus* and the *Critias*, particularly the latter. Plato, who was as much a poet as he was a philosopher, relates that Solon, the legendary lawgiver, had journeyed to Egypt at some early date in Greek history. There he met certain priests who told him that nine thousand years earlier, when Athens was the strongest and best-governed state of all, an island called Atlantis, larger than North Africa and Asia combined, lay beyond the Strait of Gibraltar. The king of Atlantis had tried to enslave Greece and Egypt, but

97

Athens led the defense, fighting on alone after all others had deserted, until one day earthquakes and floods swallowed up Atlantis and the Athenian army with it.

Plato's ancient readers apparently never thought of trying to locate Atlantis. The search began some two millenniums after he wrote—and it has never stopped. Savants like Montaigne and Voltaire seriously debated the island's existence, a learned Swede of the seventeenth century wrote no less than three volumes to demonstrate that it had been in Scandinavia, and a stream of books that prove to each author's utter satisfaction precisely where it must have been still burbles cheerfully along. The latest, at this writing, was published in the spring of 1969. Atlantis, it tells us, was a volcanic island in the Aegean Sea that blew up about 1450 B.C. Plato, of course, talks not of a pocket-sized island but of an enormous land mass, located not in the Aegean but in the Atlantic, and destroyed not nine hundred years ago but a dim nine thousand years ago—but all this leaves the author undaunted. Undauntability, however, is the strong point of most writers on Atlantis.

Atlantis solved everything. With its vast bulk filling in most of the ocean, ancient voyagers no longer had to traverse thousands of miles of open water to go from the Old World to the New; all they had to do was get over a negligible stretch on either side, and thereafter they did most of their traveling on foot. Atlantis proved so convenient that it opened up other heady possibilities besides an Egyptian migration to America. One school of thought reversed the traffic and sent Mayas scuttling eastward across this paradise to bring pyramids to the valley of the Nile.

The most dazzling idea, and the one that probably came to command the greatest number of adherents, was that Atlantis itself deserved the credit for being the fountainhead of civilization. The lost continent, it was asserted, had supported a superlatively gifted people

who, long before the disastrous total drowning, thought up things like pyramids and hieroglyphics and, migrating eastward and westward, were the common source for both Egyptian and Mayan civilization.

So far we have talked only about candidates for early crossings of the Atlantic. As far back as the sixteenth century, there were those who argued that pre-Columbian voyagers had come to the New World via the Pacific. They and their successors suggested the Chinese or Indians or Malaysians or Polynesians, and some even sent the Lost Tribes to America by way of the Far East. Others, eying the vast stretch of the Pacific, took a leaf from the book of Atlantis and conjured up a lost continent in the Pacific—Lemuria, or Mu. It once stretched, we are told, from Easter Island to the Ladrones, and its inhabitants, whose record for creativity was right up to the mark set by the Atlanteans, triumphantly carried Mu's gifts to civilization westward to India and eastward to America.

Still others offered candidates only a shade less fanciful than the inhabitants of a lost continent: Buddhist monks who had sailed off toward the east in the fifth century A.D.; Koreans escaping from Chinese tyranny; survivors of a fleet that Kublai Khan had sent out against Japan and that was almost totally destroyed in a storm; and survivors from an expedition dispatched to the Persian Gulf by Alexander the Great.

Fortunately, alongside the amateur theorizers, sober professionals—anthropologists and archaeologists— were pondering the problem of New World origins. Today, after more than a century of patient digging and collecting and observing and study, they have been able to formulate some more or less convincing conclusions. The American Indians are physically proto-Mongoloid; they must, therefore, have come from Asia. They arrived in a series of waves almost certainly by way of Alaska; the migrations took place

some ten thousand to twenty thousand years ago (new evidence may very well set the date farther back) when there was a bridge of land between Asia and America at what is now Bering Strait.* Over the centuries they filtered south, gradually climbing the standard rungs in the ladder of civilization: they learned pottery-making, farming, metallurgy, building on a large scale, writing.

As the experts amassed more and more data and sifted it, curious apparent coincidences began to crop up: certain Mayan art motifs strangely resembled certain Chinese motifs; certain pots found in Mexico looked strangely like some found in China; certain architectural elements found in Yucatán looked strangely like some found in Cambodia, and so on.

Inevitably, then, a theory arose that, long before Columbus, there was trans-Pacific contact between the Old World and the New—not a mass migration of Chinese or Israelites who subsequently turned into Mayas or Incas but traders or other visitors who brought the know-how that sparked the upward march of civilization in America. The advocates of this theory are poles apart from the devotees of a Mu or the like; they are men with a lifetime of training in the technique of gathering and evaluating evidence.

They point to motifs on Chinese bronzes of the late Chou period and similar motifs in the so-called Tajin style of Mexico; to Chinese pottery of the Han period and similar pottery found in Guatemala; to the lotus motif as treated in Buddhist art and its very similar treatment in sculptures of Yucatán; to the way figures are represented seated or "diving" in Hindu-Buddhist art and the very similar way they appear on sculpture from Palenque or Chichén Itzá. They argue that these likenesses must reflect some early impact of the Old World upon the New. A number go even further and claim that artistic influence is just the icing on the cultural cake the Old World fed to the New.

*See "The First Discovery of America" by Charlton Ogburn, Jr., in HORIZON for Winter, 1970.

Robert Heine-Geldern, a noted Austrian anthropologist who is the most radical advocate of trans-Pacific influence, has written that "future research will probably indicate that Asiatic influences of nonmaterial character were far more important than those in art and architecture. It must have been they which changed the whole structure of native society and transformed the ancient tribal cultures into civilizations more or less comparable to those of the Old World."

And so Heine-Geldern conceives of a "vast maritime expansion" of the peoples of coastal China toward the east. He has hardy Chinese mariners traveling to our shores as early as 700 B.C. By 200 B.C. he brings sailors from India into the picture, has the Chinese drop out about A.D. 200, and has Indians along with others from neighboring lands carry on so that trans-Pacific voyaging "was never really interrupted until the 9th or, perhaps, the 10th century A.D. Why it finally ended, we do not know." By the time it did, Heine-Geldern concludes, the New World had learned from Far Eastern visitors how to work metal, reckon time, write, and build monumental cities.

It is a grand theory. The trouble is that it has little more hard evidence to support it than the theories of the freewheeling amateurs. The stylistic parallels are striking—but the dates just cannot be made to coincide. A Chinese bronze of the Shang period, which ended around 1000 B.C., has an amazing resemblance to a pot found near the mouth of the Amazon—but the pot dates from A.D. 1200 at the very earliest. Motifs found in China during the Chou period do indeed resemble some of the monuments in Tajin style uncovered near Veracruz, but the Chou period ended about 200 B.C. and the Tajin monuments were built in A.D. 300 or 400. Some very ancient pottery found in Ecuador, which has been dated to 3000 B.C. and compared with Japanese pottery of the same period, seemed for a while to make a chronological fit,

but recently doubts have been raised about the age of the material from Ecuador; a date of 1000 B.C., it has been suggested, would be more reasonable.

Moreover, no Chinese or Indian object—or any object at all from the Old World—has been found in the New World in archaeological levels that date to pre-Columbian times. If Chinese or Indian traders did come regularly, they somehow left no tangible trace of their presence. Nor did they pass on to the people with whom they traded any of their useful discoveries such as the wheel, the use of iron, the domestication of cows or pigs or dogs or horses, or the planting of wheat (the New World fed on corn). Finally, there is the matter of Chinese seamanship. For a very long while the Chinese preferred to let others do their ocean hauling. As a matter of fact, the first securely dated Chinese ocean voyage did not take place until as late as the fifteenth century A.D.

Yet the puzzling parallels are there, too many and too close to be explained away as mere coincidences. Surely occasional visitors must have come. The winds and currents of the North Pacific trend eastward. Any craft caught helpless in their embrace can easily be carried across the ocean; records show, for example, that between 1775 and 1875 about twenty Japanese junks were blown to the west coast of America.

If Japanese junks in the last century, why not Chinese or Indian or Malaysian ones in preceding centuries? No question about it, a certain number must have ended a storm-tossed journey on this side of the Pacific. Perhaps a few of the bolder spirits among their crews risked the long sail back home, but most must have chosen to settle down where they landed. Eventually they either died out or were wholly absorbed, leaving behind only tantalizing hints of their presence.

What about the South Pacific? If the North Pacific had the winds and currents to bring people willy-nilly across to America, the South Pacific had the mariners to make the trip of their

own free will. The South Pacific is a world of multitudinous far-flung fragments of land; the name "Polynesia" derives from Greek elements that mean "many islands." Thanks to the maritime enterprise of the Polynesians, most of them were already populated by the time Europeans arrived on the scene, including those separated by great stretches of water.

The standard craft of these seamen was a canoe balanced by an outrigger and driven by a rig enabling it to travel to a certain extent against the wind. For transporting large groups they used double canoes made up of two hulls yoked by booms and with a platform spanning the space in between, an embryonic version of the catamarans that are the latest wrinkle in yacht design today. These ran large enough to accommodate as many as two hundred and fifty persons. Piloting such unsophisticated vessels fearlessly and with consummate ability, the Polynesians managed to reach almost every bit of land in the South Pacific. Their original home seems to have been southeastern Asia. From there they filtered through Micronesia or Melanesia and, at no very remote age, perhaps the fifth century A.D., made their debut in western Polynesia. The period of their most active colonization was probably as late as the twelfth to the fourteenth centuries.

These voyages were recalled in many a Polynesian legend, and anthropologists soon concluded that the Polynesian skipper, by using every primitive means of navigation available—observation not only of the stars but of wind and wave direction, of the flight of migratory birds, and of the distinctive clouds that hang above islands—could sail for weeks over trackless ocean to make a landfall on a tiny target. They credited him in effect with

OVERLEAF: *All the navigators shown on this teeming map of our hemisphere have been championed as the original bringers of culture to (or from) prehistoric America. When, how, why, and if they did it remains in dispute.*

Voyagers All:

"American" Indians

Buddhists

Koreans

Chinese

Indians

Greeks

Polynesians

Malaysians

Peruvians

int Brendan

Vikings

Lost Tribes of Israel

Phoenicians

Columbus

Mayas

Egyptians

being able to set and hold a course as accurately as Europeans equipped with compass, log, and a knowledge of celestial navigation. Accordingly, they claimed that the Polynesians were the first people to have intentionally made their way over, if not all of the Pacific, at least a good part of it.

The Polynesians were as fine a race of seamen as the world has ever known. But they were not miracle workers. Some years ago, Andrew Sharp in his *Ancient Voyagers in Polynesia* took a close look at all the available evidence and demonstrated that they conducted regular two-way traffic over three hundred miles of open water at the most and usually only one to two hundred— in other words, voyages of but a day or two. Their fast-stepping canoes covered one hundred miles in twenty-four hours in good weather, and this in itself is achievement enough to place the Polynesians high on the honor roll of maritime races. But no regular traffic between points farther apart is recorded, for it was utterly beyond their powers. Stars offer scant help on north-south courses and no help at all during the day or on cloudy nights; wind and wave direction can change in an instant; and no skipper dares to count on steady sightings of distinctive birds or cloud formations.

Polynesians certainly did reach and populate the shores of Hawaii and Easter Island and other remote spots, but the founding fathers did not navigate their way there—they were brought by chance, with ladies luckily present to be pressed into service as founding mothers. Polynesian legend is full of stories of canoes blown by storm to far places, and many instances were noted by the Europeans who lived among the islanders before traditional ways had changed.

An even more significant contributor to haphazard long-distance colonization was war. War among Polynesians was usually fought to the death, and the losing side, faced with certain extinction, understandably preferred to load themselves, their goods, and some

essential food plants aboard their canoes and take their chances that Heaven would direct them to an empty piece of land.

Did any Polynesians ever get blown clear across the Pacific? Since they were carried as far as Easter Island, a good thousand miles to the east of their nearest brethren, might they not have been swept on for another two thousand miles, right to the coast of South America? Those who think so point to the squashes and gourds, native to America, that are found in Polynesia— but the seeds could just as well have been carried by birds through the air as by Polynesians returning in boats. For a while it was believed that the New World's staple food, corn, might itself have been brought from Asia by Polynesians, but the discovery of corn pollen in America in levels that go back at least sixty thousand years put an end to that.

Only one agricultural product has so far weathered all the storms of scholarly controversy, the sweet potato. It is native to America and is called in Peruvian tongues *kumar;* it is found in Polynesia, and the general Polynesian word for it is *kumara.* An obvious conclusion is that Polynesians not only reached South America but made it safely back, taking with them one of the most useful items the New World had to offer, name and all.

But a few saw it just the other way around. They held that it was South Americans who brought the sweet potato to Polynesia. This was for years just another theory, more or less buried in the obscurity of professional books and journals. Then Thor Heyerdahl moved the argument to the public stage and stepped into the spotlight.

The Polynesians, Heyerdahl reminded everyone, were not the only gifted sailors in the area. The inhabitants of the west coast of South America were no slouches; they were able to cover great distances with their favored type of craft, a seagoing raft made of light balsa logs. Moreover, the winds

and currents between South America and Polynesia in the warmer latitudes are prevailingly easterly: a Polynesian would have to buck both to get to South America, whereas a Peruvian needed merely to raise sail and coast. To clinch the argument, Heyerdahl made his celebrated grand gesture: he built a balsa sailing raft, the famed *Kon-Tiki,* shoved off from Callao in Peru, and 101 days and 4,300 miles later fetched up on one of the islands in the Tuamotu group. Having launched the *Kon-Tiki* so successfully, Heyerdahl then launched his pet theory, that the Polynesian islands were settled by South Americans who had been carried there by wind and current as he had.

As things turned out, it was easier to keep the *Kon-Tiki* afloat than the theory. Heyerdahl marshaled what seemed to be an impressive list of proofs. By the time his opponents had finished taking pot shots at them, hardly a one was left standing. Moreover, one of his many challengers, Eric de Bisschop, who was even wiser than Heyerdahl in the ways of seagoing rafts, took it upon himself to demonstrate that a raft could just as well make the voyage in the opposite direction.

To cross vast expanses of open water in little boats seems to have been De Bisschop's greatest joy in life. In 1937 he sailed a thirty-seven-foot double canoe from Hawaii across the Pacific to Australia, through the Torres Strait, across the Indian Ocean, around the Cape of Good Hope, up the Atlantic to the Strait of Gibraltar, and into the Mediterranean. In 1956, exasperated by all the publicity the *Kon-Tiki* and her skipper were getting, he decided, at the age of sixty-five, to demonstrate that, despite Heyerdahl's talk of winds and currents permitting a raft to voyage only from east to west, one could also do it from west to east.

De Bisschop's answer to the *Kon-Tiki* was the *Tahiti Nui,* a raft of bamboo logs. In November of 1956 he left from Tahiti, holding a course due south into lower latitudes, where he knew he had a chance to pick up westerlies. By

May he was near the Juan Fernández Islands, no more than five hundred miles from Valparaiso, his intended destination. Here he ran into a series of vicious storms; the raft became too battered to be trusted, and he and his crew reluctantly abandoned it and allowed a Chilean cruiser to carry them to safety.

A year later he had readied the *Tahiti Nui II,* and on April 13, 1958, he sailed from Callao to repeat Heyerdahl's feat. But the sea is a dangerous gaming partner, and De Bisschop had gambled once too often: four months after their departure he and his crew ended up on a reef off Rakahanga in the Northern Cooks. His companions did their best to save him, but he was dead by the time they got him on the beach. Nevertheless, he had made his point: with ordinary luck a seagoing raft could get from Polynesia to South America and back.

But that was all he or Heyerdahl had proved: that a raft *could* make it. And whatever rafts—or canoes—ever did, did so by accident. So far as we know to this day, the first man to have laid and followed a course from one side of the Pacific to the other was Ferdinand Magellan in 1519. As for the Atlantic, it, too, *could* have been crossed by primitive craft. But so far as we know, no one intentionally sailed across it before Columbus.

As it happens, the first planned ocean crossing on record took place in the Indian Ocean in the second century B.C., but the voyage involved no great feat of seamanship. It was, in fact, almost humdrum.

Perhaps as early as the third millennium B.C., sailors were plying the waters of the Indian Ocean between the western shores of India and the Persian Gulf. By at least the first millennium B.C. they were making their way to the east coast of Africa and the mouth of the Red Sea, carrying precious cargoes of Chinese silks, Far Eastern spices, and other luxury goods. The traffic, extremely lucrative, was largely in the hands of Indian and Arab seamen, and they had no intention of letting anyone else in on it. And so for centuries they kept to themselves a priceless trade secret, the behavior of the monsoon winds. These, with splendid convenience, blow from the northeast during the winter and then shift to precisely the opposite quarter for the summer; sailing vessels were thus ensured a fair wind for both legs of the journey.

But about 120 B.C. the secret finally leaked out. One day a half-drowned sailor was brought to the court of Ptolemy VII at Alexandria. After being nursed back to health and taught Greek, he gave out the story that he was an Indian, the sole survivor of his crew, and he offered to prove it by showing anyone the king picked out the way back to his home. Eudoxus of Cyzicus, a well-known explorer was in town at the time and the choice fell on him; under government auspices, he twice sailed to India and back.

There was nothing to it. The route had been traveled by generations of anonymous skippers before him, he knew what he would find at the other end, and he was guaranteed a fair wind each way. During the homeward leg of the second voyage a bit of excitement developed when he was carried farther south than he expected and ended up on the coast of Africa below Cape Guardafui. But he made friends with the natives in the best explorer tradition by giving them strange delicacies (bread, wine, and dried figs did the trick), and even picked up a few words of their tongue.

Eudoxus's troubles began only after he got back. Both times he had landed with an invaluable cargo of spices and perfumes and gems, only to see Ptolemy's customs agents confiscate all of it. In a way they posed for him the same problem that the closing of the Suez Canal does for Mediterranean shippers today. His solution anticipated theirs: he readied an expedition to sail all around Africa from west to east and thereby bypass Egypt. He fitted it out to the nines, even taking aboard a number of dancing girls; whether for the harems of Indian rajahs or to help while away the long hours at sea, we cannot know. He sailed from Cadiz, but when he got as far as the Atlantic coast of Morocco, a mutiny sent him back. Undaunted, he equipped a second expedition just as carefully, set sail, and vanished without a trace.

So in compiling the list of recorded transatlantic voyages, we start with Eudoxus. Then, skipping over the legendary voyage of the sixth-century Irish Saint Brendan, we make a leap of more than a thousand years to the Vikings. In the tenth century Eric the Red led a group of colonists to Greenland, and thereafter Viking craft shuttled regularly between Norway and Iceland and Greenland. To be sure, the Atlantic crossing at this point is narrow, involving only some two hundred miles of open water, but it requires courage and seamanship beyond the call of crossings in lower latitudes. Eric's son Leif pushed on from Greenland to "Vinland," generally thought to be in Labrador or Newfoundland or Nova Scotia, but he very likely followed the coasts as much as he could rather than a course straight over the sea. From the Vikings we jump half a millennium to Columbus and Magellan.

The list is short and is not likely to grow any longer. But of course the list of nonauthenticated voyages grows annually. With the successful voyage of the *Ra II,* Heyerdahl has now added to it the ancient Egyptians who used to sail papyrus boats on the Nile—though never, so far as anyone knows, on the open sea. Not long ago, in a dispatch datelined Warsaw, *The New York Times* reported that "Polish scientists are planning to sail a primitive 82-foot boat from Casablanca to Mexico to prove that North Africans could have settled the new world 4,000 years ago." And, who knows? Maybe next year the Russians will launch an expedition to find Atlantis.

Lionel Casson's latest book is Ships and Seamanship in the Ancient World.

The Heyerdahl Paradox

This dauntless sailor—who cannot sail—is a fugitive from modernity;
yet what he proved with his seagoing rafts may be as relevant to
the problems of space travel and pollution as it is to ancient history

If they ever get around to giving a Nobel Prize for Creative Eccentricity—and why not?—an obvious candidate for the first award would be Thor Heyerdahl, explorer, scholar, author, and indomitable partisan of ancient man. Still, the word "eccentric" may be misleading, suggesting that Heyerdahl has an angle of vision that is (dread fate!) irrelevant.

The contrary is true. In looking backward, Heyerdahl is astonishingly up-to-date; in circling the globe in primitive vessels he has, paradoxically, given us a glimpse of the future. To mention one example, by using a polyglot crew in his *Ra* voyages, he has demonstrated the feasibility of using multinational teams in extended space travel. (But more of that later.)

Or, to cite another example, Heyerdahl has arguably done more than anyone else, save Jacques Yves Cousteau, the underwater explorer, to publicize the doleful fact that we are poisoning our oceans, turning the seas around us into lethal sinks of pollution. (More of that later, too.)

The interesting thing is that both of

The Norwegian anthropologist Thor Heyerdahl crossed the Atlantic from Morocco in the Ra II, *opposite, a papyrus boat similar to those used by ancient Egyptian sailors.*

these important—and manifestly relevant—achievements were incidental benefits of ventures that were scorned as quixotic or suicidal, or both. Before his epic *Kon-Tiki* expedition in 1947, Heyerdahl was repeatedly warned that he was foolishly risking his own life,

Thor Heyerdahl

and the lives of five Scandinavian shipmates, by attempting to cross the Pacific in a balsa raft. Likewise, before he embarked on the *Ra I* in 1969—this time with a crew of six from as many countries—he was solemnly assured by qualified experts that papyrus, the reed from which his boat was made, would disintegrate after a few weeks at sea, just as it did in experimental tubs.

Heyerdahl, of course, proved that these forecasts, proffered with vast

certitude, were false. The *Kon-Tiki* odyssey, moreover, was not simply a fluke; there have been no fewer than ten subsequent raft voyages across the Pacific, as of 1970, with all hands surviving. When the *Ra I*, listing badly after being pounded by successive storms, was abandoned just short of its goal in the New World, Heyerdahl was undiscouraged. Less than a year later, he was back again with the *Ra II*, departing once more from the Moroccan port of Safi, and this time his papyrus craft—built by Aymara Indians from Lake Titicaca, unlike the *Ra I*, which was stitched together by African tribesmen from Lake Chad—triumphantly completed the 3,270-mile Atlantic crossing in fifty-seven days.

In the process, Heyerdahl did two things. First he proved that vessels made of balsa and papyrus were seaworthy, and that even a crew of landlubbers could survive on them in oceanic voyages. This suggests that similar trips could have occurred in remote times; whatever his own beliefs may be, Heyerdahl has never claimed that his ocean voyages themselves proved any more than this. Nevertheless, others have cited his feats as proof for the "diffusionist" theory—the theory, namely, that what we call civilization had essentially a single

On his famous balsa raft, the Kon-Tiki, left, Heyerdahl voyaged 4,300 miles from Peru to Polynesia in 1947 to prove, in his words, "that ancient Peru could have contributed to Polynesian culture." In 1969 Heyerdahl made his first attempt to sail a forty-foot reed craft—named "Ra" after the Egyptian sun god—across the Atlantic to Barbados, this time to prove that the ancient Near East could have contributed to New World civilization. Opposite, the Ra's crew included, from left, an American, a Mexican, a Russian, a Norwegian (Heyerdahl), an African from Chad, an Italian, and, not seen, an Egyptian.

source in the ancient Near East, from which it spread like the widening circle of water stirred by a pebble tossed into a pond.

But Heyerdahl did more than cross the ocean. He has also entertained the world. No one knows exactly how many copies of *Kon-Tiki* have been sold—the accepted estimate is twenty million—but there is small doubt that his first best seller, published in 1950, is one of the most widely translated books of all time, possibly outranked only by the Bible. It has appeared in more than sixty languages, including Tamil, Gujarati, Singalese, Telugi, Marathi, and Esperanto. *Aku-Aku*, the narrative of his Easter Island explorations during 1955, was also a runaway best seller, and all the signs indicate that his latest popular book, *The Ra Expeditions*, fortified, as *Kon-Tiki* was, by the success of a documentary film of the venture, will gladden hearts on Publishers' Row.

For Heyerdahl, this dazzling acclaim has been a mixed blessing. To be sure, the royalties have made it possible for him to pursue his own work independently; but among scholars, Heyerdahl is suspect, for the seriousness of his purpose has been obscured by his celebrity. The press has cast him as a carefree Sinbad cavorting on strange

floating objects, summoning up slithery spirits from the vasty deep. A whole dimension of Heyerdahl's personality has been lost—his brooding melancholy and his profound distrust of the modern era.

He lives in a medieval Italian village, and buys hardly anything in cans or bottles. He owns no television, has never learned to drive, and works in an ancient tower that is without electricity. His aversion to gadgetry dates from his early manhood, when he left Norway to live for a year like a savage on a remote Polynesian island. But perhaps most startling of all, the celebrated skipper of the *Kon-Tiki,* the conqueror of the Atlantic in a paper boat—this latter-day Viking cannot sail.

As I learned when I visited him recently at his home, Colla Micheri, on an olive-cloaked bluff overlooking the coast of Liguria.

One's first impression is of wary reserve, of a person posted with "No Trespassing" signs, like those one sees along the dirt road that climbs to his house. We were in his library, surrounded by a multitude of editions of *Kon-Tiki*, and I had complimented him on combining an interest in ethnology and ecology with superlative seamanship.

"Thank you," Heyerdahl replied, "but I must correct you when you praise my seamanship. I'm not a sailor —no one takes it seriously when I say so, but it's true. I have a friend who has a sailboat, and I can't take it from one end of the bay below us to the other. I am an expedition leader; I get a navigator to do the sailing.

"But that is the point of what I have tried to do. I load my vessels with people who know nothing about the sea. Abdullah [the African tribesman who was in charge of building the *Ra I*] didn't even know that the ocean was salty. I am trying to show that people exaggerate the difficulty of crossing the ocean on what may seem like a primitive vessel.

"Actually," he pursued, "they are not so primitive. I myself have a distrust of anything that is heavier than water. I get nervous on boats made of wood or metal—I'd much rather be on something unsinkable, like balsa or papyrus. A wooden hull is really a most risky venture."

As we talked, I took a closer look at the man. He seems ten years younger than his fifty-seven years. His eyes are polar blue, he does not smile readily, and there is a flatness to his slightly accented English—the sentences can come out with the precise impersonality

of a computer print-out. But one has an immediate sense of formidable competence and of directed purpose. I remarked that it must have been more difficult to sail with a mixed crew, on the *Ra* voyages, than with other Scandinavians (four Norwegians and a solitary Swede) aboard the *Kon-Tiki*.

"On the contrary, it was easier with a crew that had nothing in common— race, religion, class, or nationality. That gave me the most pleasure, to see how well we worked as a team, even though we had to use three common languages." English, French, and Italian were all spoken by Heyerdahl, by Georges Sourial, a Copt from Cairo, and by Dr. Santiago Genovés, a Mexican anthropologist.

"It was more difficult on *Kon-Tiki*, and I'll tell you why. On your first day on a raft, you're still a guest, very well-mannered. But this does not last more than three days, and then it is like an unending house party in which you are trapped with the others. After a month, you get what I call 'expedition fever.' You lose all sense of proportion, small irritants blow up into terrible quarrels. In my log, I had to keep detailed records of every minor dispute, so that when a bigger fight came along, I'd know all the facts.

"Well, if you're all from the same background, as we were on *Kon-Tiki*, you are too liable to relax. Anger is too easily expressed. With different backgrounds, you stay on guard, almost as if you were an ambassador. It is much, much easier with a multinational crew, believe me."

Heyerdahl called my attention to a report made by the Soviet member of the crew, Yuri A. Senkevich, who was the ship's doctor, to the Orbital International Laboratory, or OIL, a world organization concerned with space travel. Senkevich said that on the basis of his own experience aboard the *Ra I* and *II* he was convinced of the feasibility of multinational space flight, and this conclusion had the potent endorsement of the Russian Academy of Sciences (the president of the academy had proposed Senkevich as a crew member when Heyerdahl requested a Soviet volunteer).

If the shipboard harmony gave Heyerdahl pleasure, the filth in the ocean caused him the deepest distress. "It was shocking, absolutely shocking," he said. "On our *Kon-Tiki* trip in the Pacific, we didn't see a piece of man-made material for weeks on end, not a bottle, not a can. But on the Atlantic, hardly a day passed without our finding a plastic bottle. Imagine, we couldn't brush our teeth in ocean water —you would get a mouthful of oil."

In his *Ra II* journey, Heyerdahl kept a day-by-day record of visible pollution and found that on forty-three out of fifty-seven days at sea there was human garbage around the ship, little of it visible from the loftier decks of tankers and ocean liners. His melancholy pollution log was submitted to the United Nations (whose flag both *Ra*'s had flown), along with a chemical analysis of noxious samples. His words are worth quoting: "It is not the objective of the *Ra* expedition to draw biological or ecological conclusions from our observations. Our intention is merely to call attention to observations virtually forced upon us. Yet there is no doubt that the time is past when ocean pollution is a mere offense to human esthetics; if left unchecked, it can hardly avoid affecting the future world economy."

Heyerdahl organized the expedition to get a glimpse of man's past and found himself floating into the oily future. "I was frankly scared," he confessed, "but as horrible as it is, this may be a problem that unites mankind." He is now a frequent speaker at world conferences on pollution.

All the same, the filth did not take Heyerdahl wholly by surprise; it served

At the foot of the Pyramids, left, Heyerdahl supervises construction of the Ra I *in 1969, basing the design on Egyptian tomb reliefs. With him are three shipwrights from Africa's Lake Chad, one of the few places where the ancient Mediterranean art of reed shipbuilding survives. Although reed ships are unsinkable, the Chad method of construction, using small separate reed bundles, proved inadequate. Raging storms some six hundred miles from Barbados virtually shredded away the* Ra's *starboard side, opposite, forcing Heyerdahl to abandon ship. He immediately began planning a second expedition.*

rather to confirm his bleaker views of our imperfect era. Indeed, his career can be seen as a series of attempted escapes from the pervasive prison of the modern world—beginning in 1937, when he decided to live as a Stone Age man in Polynesia. He was twenty-two at the time, a fresh graduate (in zoology) of Oslo University; he had fallen in love with and proposed to a pretty Norwegian girl, on condition that she, too, would abandon bourgeois comforts for the Stone Age. He duly departed, with his savings and his bride of a week, for the island of Fatu Hiva in the Marquesas, taking a machete and a cooking pot but little else (even matches and medicine were left behind).

The experiment lasted a year. The couple contended with sickness, hunger, and poisonous centipedes before finally admitting defeat and returning to Norway. His first book, *In Search of Paradise* (as yet not translated into English), grew out of the experience, which was to shape the rest of his life. When I saw a copy of the book, in a proud place of honor on the crowded shelf, I asked why he had searched for paradise. He replied reflectively.

"When I was in high school, I first began to feel that civilization was on a calamity course. So when I was able to,

I went to Polynesia to live as a Stone Age man, without a cash economy, surviving by harvesting fruits and by fishing and hunting without modern weapons. I wanted to see civilization from the outside and I did. It taught me more than all my years at school.

"I began to believe that for the last five thousand years the brain has made no progress at all, that all we have done is to alter the environment. Seeing it from the outside, I could find no plan in civilization—just a matter of changing things, inventing things, but without a plan. In a way, you know, I was the first hippie, thirty years ago.

"So I am not among those who criticize the young. Instead I put my faith in them, as people who have jumped off the train when it is clearly leaving the track. There is an equilibrium in human nature, and if this generation goes too far in one direction, the next may pull the pendulum back."

It was by now late afternoon, and Heyerdahl excused himself to return to the old birdcatcher's tower that he uses as a study. I was taken to the door of his fortress-like home by his wife Yvonne (not his companion on the Polynesian island; his first marriage ended in an amicable divorce and he remarried in 1949). Peeping from behind a doorway were two of his three

daughters, their hair as blonde as the wood of the Scandinavian furniture in the ingeniously restored interior.

As I walked down a cobblestone path to my car, I had a chance to get a better look at Colla Micheri, a medieval hamlet shaded with pine and coated with ivy. There is a sundial in the piazza, with a weathered motto on it that can be roughly rendered, "Can I tell you the time? Of course I can:/It is time for work, for an honest man." Everywhere there were sheep, chickens, and goats; farmers on the estate make their own cheese, wine, and oil. A pink church bears an inscription commemorating the visit by His Holiness Pius VII in 1814. A moss-covered Roman road crosses the piazza.

When Heyerdahl first saw the village, during a holiday visit to Italy in 1958, he was instantly ensnared and quickly arranged to buy and restore most of it, moving his family into the then half-ruined patrician's house. As he explained to his biographer and boyhood friend Arnold Jacoby: "I knew straightaway that I had come to stay.... Here, at Colla Micheri, was everything I had dreamed of, palms and blue sea, pines and orange groves and, nearby, snow-covered mountains sheltering friendly shepherds and vine cultivators from the northern winds."

No doubt it was another attempted escape by an unabashed romantic, and ironically, Colla Micheri looks down on the resort town of Alassio on the Italian Riveria, with its seasonal honky-tonk and tasteless souvenir stands. Complete escape is impossible, and yet the very attempt has its infectious delights.

Heyerdahl has never lacked volunteers for his expeditions, nor have any crew members regretted signing up. Most, in fact, have been caught up in the currents of the experience, like the queer vessels they manned. This was confirmed to me through an agreeable coincidence. Not long after seeing Heyerdahl, I happened to be in Mexico City and noticed an announcement of a lecture to be given by Dr. Santiago Genovés, with the tantalizing title "The *Ra* Voyages: More Adventure than Science?" And so I went.

Dr. Genovés, short, peppery, and seemingly fluent in every known language, had wound up on the papyrus raft thanks to a chance meeting with Heyerdahl in which the Mexican anthropologist had said, half in jest, that he would join the crew on a week's notice. As it happened, the Mexican who was originally supposed to be on the *Ra I* suddenly fell ill, and Heyer-dahl had anxiously cabled Genovés from Morocco, giving him seven days to get on board. He became the expedition's quartermaster, though he had no experience at sea, and took charge of filling the ship's 160 amphorae, which had been molded in an ancient Egyptian pattern, with such morsels as bread baked according to a similarly ancient recipe.

The hall was filled as Dr. Genovés began his illustrated talk by lamenting the way in which the press had stressed the stunt aspects of the *Ra* voyages, "as if we were like those boys who bicycle to Patagonia or try to cross the English Channel in a bathtub." There were more serious aspects, he pointed out, because the papyrus vessels were literally "little laboratories of human behavior," with the crew like so many white mice.

Dr. Genovés, it developed, had been busy testing the behavior of the floating mice. Was sexual privation a problem? No, his studies indicated, because the overwhelming concern with sheer survival diminished sexual impulses. He also took tests to measure the compatibility of the crew under stress conditions, and discovered that during the trips, largely with the same people, the lines of affection and hostility were not consistent, suggesting that group emotions are not as constant as one might suppose. All of these findings were being prepared for subsequent publication.

I later learned that this spin-off effect of the Heyerdahl expeditions had ample precedent on the *Kon-Tiki,* whose voyage reshaped the future of each crew member. There was Bengt Danielsson, the red-bearded Swede who joined the crew at the last moment—he happened to be canoeing in Peru at the time—and who became smitten with Tahiti, where the voyagers wound up. He settled on the island, won a doctorate with a thesis on native life, and eventually was appointed director of the National Ethnographic Museum in Stockholm.

There was Herman Watzinger, an engineer whose specialty was refrigeration. He liked Peru, moved there, and became Norwegian Consul General, going into the business of building cold-storage plants for the Latin-American fishing industry. There was Erik Hesselberg, a boyhood chum of Heyerdahl's, who wrote his own account of the voyage and illustrated it with impish cartoons. The book had a European success, and he later became the decorator of *Kon-Tiki* restaurants around the world. There was Torstein Raaby, who had fought alongside

Heyerdahl's happy crew, left, stands atop the cabin of the sturdy Ra II *in July, 1970, as it makes its way toward Barbados, after covering 3,270 sea miles in fifty-seven days. The* Ra II *was built by Indians from Bolivia's Lake Titicaca, where reed shipbuilding differs in very few details from ancient Mediterranean methods, another "astonishing fact," says Heyerdahl, suggesting contact between the ancient Near East and America. Opposite, he is joined by his wife and daughters at Bridgetown, Barbados, the day he completed the voyage that a Pharaoh's seamen might have made three millenniums ago.*

Heyerdahl during World War II as a Norwegian commando in Finnmark; his lectures on the voyage financed his education as a radio engineer. Raaby went to the Arctic to man a radio station and died there in 1964 while leading an expedition to the North Pole.

Finally, there was Knut Haugland, who had parachuted (like Heyerdahl) into occupied Norway. Haugland, in characteristic circumstances, was to become director of the Kon-Tiki Museum. After the voyage, Heyerdahl offered his raft as a gift to the Norwegian government; the offer was politely declined. Three Oslo businessmen then provided funds for an improvised shelter for the *Kon-Tiki,* and the visitor response in the first few years was sufficiently astonishing to persuade the government to reconsider. A state-supported museum was built, appropriately located next to the structure enclosing Fridtjof Nansen's polar schooner, *Fram.* It is today the most popular museum in Norway, drawing a quarter of a million visitors a year.

Against this background of fulfillment, it would be pleasant to report that Heyerdahl's audacious theories about the voyages of ancient man have carried the day in his academic battles, but this is far from the case. Some early critics were won over, notably Dr.

Samuel K. Lothrop of Harvard, who once doubted the seaworthiness of balsa rafts but who later wrote to Heyerdahl, "As the years go by, I feel more and more inclined to accept your viewpoint without reservation, and I greatly admire the scholarship on which it is based."

Others, who question his theory of diffusion, nevertheless concede that he has thrown fresh light on the problem. Dr. Michael D. Coe, chairman of the Anthropology Department at Yale and a nondiffusionist, credits Heyerdahl with stimulating the first concerted archaeological attack on Polynesian prehistory. "He doesn't try to control the conclusions of scholars who take part in his expeditions, he learns from his mistakes," says Coe, "and he is unquestionably a refreshing figure."

Indeed, considering that his essential theory is frequently considered entirely daft, the wonder is that he has any support at all. His theory came to him during his crucial year's stay in Polynesia in 1937-38 when he noticed that the ocean breakers rolled on only one side of the islands—the eastern side. At the same time he learned of Tiki, the legendary god-king who was supposed to have come from the east as the ancestor of today's islanders.

So it occurred to Heyerdahl that Polynesia could have been reached from mainland South America, four thousand miles away, a notion that almost all qualified scholars rejected as an absurdity. The accepted view was that Polynesia was settled from Asia, which the linguistic links between the areas strongly suggested. But Heyerdahl never contended that Polynesia was peopled solely from South America; he argued instead that the region was a melting pot, a meeting place of diverse cultures. On linguistic evidence alone, he likes to point out, it could be maintained that the United States was colonized only by Britons.

He became interested in other possibilities. A separate wave of migrants could have come to Polynesia from the northwest coast of America, explaining some apparent affinities between the Indians of the Pacific Northwest and the islanders. More controversial yet, he speculated that Old World voyagers might have reached the New World long before Columbus, accounting for the prevalent Indian myths about bearded white gods. But this is fairly nebulous, and the notion has unfortunate echoes of the many crank theories about the lost continents of Atlantis and Mu and the Lost Tribes of Israel.

Besides, how did those ancient voyagers manage to cross the ocean? The obvious objection was put to Heyerdahl again and again when he found himself in America in 1946 with a manuscript under his arm that nobody would read, much less publish. In an encounter with Dr. Herbert Spinden, then director of the Brooklyn Museum, Heyerdahl was brusquely informed that none of the peoples of South America ever reached the Pacific islands. "Do you know why?" demanded Spinden. "They had no boats!"

"They had rafts," Heyerdahl somewhat weakly replied, "you know, balsa-wood rafts."

"Well, you can try a trip from Peru to the Pacific islands on a balsa-wood raft."

With the *Kon-Tiki* voyage, Heyerdahl silenced some of the laughter by proving that the raft, if not elegant, was nonetheless seaworthy. The same purpose prompted the *Ra* voyages; Heyerdahl decided upon a reed boat because this was a type of vessel common to both the Old and New Worlds in ancient times. Without being committed to any specific theory of diffusion, he wanted to see whether an Atlantic crossing could have been made in such a boat. As with the *Kon-Tiki*,

the experts were uniformly discouraging. The president of the Egyptian Papyrus Institute tested bits of reed in a laboratory tank and reported to Heyerdahl that the papyrus disintegrated in sea water. ("I thought for myself," Heyerdahl remarked, "that he might as well have tested a piece of iron and he would have come to the conclusion that the *Queen Mary* would sink.")

But to his lay admirers, scholarly arguments are beside the point. It is the man himself who is fascinating. He is a throwback to a largely extinct breed of explorers, to men like Burton and Livingstone, Scott and Shackleton, or his own compatriots, Nansen and Amundsen. Like them, he goes his own way, he bets his life on his beliefs, with no vast bureaucracy to cosset him, and then he writes compelling books and articles about his adventures. He is the anti-astronaut.

Such flourishes as building a papyrus boat beneath the Pyramids of Giza smack of showmanship, but he has avoided blatant gimmickry. In 1969 American space officials proposed connecting special antennae to the *Ra I* so that the crew could exchange greetings with the Apollo astronauts on their moon flight. Heyerdahl wasn't buying; he politely said no, remarking to a re-

porter, "If I have to fix those weird antennae on that boat, it won't look as if I came from ancient Egypt, I tell you that!"

Recently I chanced to have lunch with Dr. Gordon Ekholm of the American Museum of Natural History, a distinguished proponent of the diffusionist theory. Heyerdahl's name came up, and Ekholm beamed. He told me of receiving a radiogram via ham operators from the *Ra I,* signed by Heyerdahl and Genovés and reading, "Seven men with Olmec beards approaching the New World some millennia too late to influence Olmec culture." (The Olmecs were the creators of the earliest high civilization in Mexico.)

Later, Ekholm supplied me with a copy of the radiogram. As I held it, I thought of those seven men on that ludicrous paper boat, blazoned with the emblem of an ancient sun god. And I asked myself where I would rather be —on a chill spacecraft heading toward a lifeless moon or planet, or aboard that bouncing raft skippered by a nonsailor. It didn't take me long to make up my mind.

A newspaperman and political reporter by profession, Karl E. Meyer often turns his eye on the ancient world. The Pleasures of Archaeology *is his latest book.*

Two By
Ogden Nash

Through four decades, from 1930 until his death last May, this gentle and modest master of humorous verse kept an army of readers bewitched, bemused, and begging for more. His comments on the passing scene—generous helpings of reason flavored with marvelously audacious rhymes and laced with puns—were products of the most exacting craftsmanship, and so distinctively his own as to defy all attempts at imitation. The poems on these pages will appear in a new collection of his verse—the twenty-first—to be published this spring by Little, Brown and entitled *The Old Dog Barks Backwards.*

THE REJECTED PORTRAIT

Mr. Danvers in the chair
Runs his fingers through his hair,
Gives his chest a manly heave
And smoothes the wrinkles in his sleeve.
The empty backside of the canvas
A mirror is to Mr. Danvers
In which he may with cunning ferrety
Rehearse his meeting with posterity.
He must his part as brilliant play
As a Gielgud or Olivier.
Just what should the expression be
To catch the essential Mr. D.?
Emotions stumble across his face
Like kids in a potato race.
See how his facial muscles work
Lest whimsical smile become a smirk.
Now he is frowning, now he's quizzical,
Now meditative or metaphysical.
Watch him in fleeting roles consecutive,
Athlete, musician, stern executive.
Oddly, of all his parts the oddest
Is that in which he's playing modest.
The painter, who's been there before,
He knows what mummeries to ignore;
Somehow, from under each mad grimace
He excavates a human face.
Then where's the genuine Mr. Danvers?
Not in the chair, but on the canvas.

THE SLIPSHOD SCHOLAR GETS AROUND TO GREECE

I sing of the ancient Greeks.

They had magnificent physiques.

They were also intellectual Titans,

And wore chlamydes and chitons.

Their minds were serene unless too much success induced *hubris,*

In which case the gods rendered them lugubrous.

They were pre-eminent in art and science,

And in their pottery they anticipated faïence.

Indeed they were our precursors in many ways, just think how
their man Homer did Milton and Tennyson precurse;

Because he could not think of a rhyme for orange he invented
blank verse.

Even the stock exchange reflects their far-off light;

Had the Greeks not bequeathed us their language, brokers would
be trading not in AT&T but in American Distantsound & Distantwrite.

If the Greeks had never existed who would have been the most annoyed?

Freud.

Without their drama where would he have uncovered all those complexes,

His pop-plexes and mom-plexes?

The path of Oedipus into the annals of analysis was straight, Electra's
rather more tortuous.

I shall try to map it for you though I may evoke offended cries of
De mortuis.

Electra persuaded her brother, Orestes, to murder their mother,
Clytemnestra, who had persuaded her lover, Aegisthus, to
murder Agamemnon, their father, whom Electra loved like
billy-o,

And Orestes did in fact murder Clytemnestra and her lover with
classic punctilio.

Thus was Agamemnon avenged and his adulterous slayers eradicated.

The Greek words for Electra were accessory before the fact, but
Dr. Freud and I think of her simply as a daughter who was
over-daddycated.

The First Feminist

In 1792 Mary Wollstonecraft wrote
a book to prove that her sex was as intelligent
as the other: thus did feminism
come into the world. Right on, Ms. Mary!

The first person—male or female—to speak at any length and to any effect about woman's rights was Mary Wollstonecraft. In 1792, when her *Vindication of the Rights of Woman* appeared, Mary was a beautiful spinster of thirty-three who had made a successful career for herself in the publishing world of London. This accomplishment was rare enough for a woman in that day. Her manifesto, at once impassioned and learned, was an achievement of real originality. The book electrified the reading public and made Mary famous. The core of its argument is simple: "I wish to see women neither heroines nor brutes; but reasonable creatures," Mary wrote. This ancestress of the Women's Liberation Movement did not demand day-care centers or an end to woman's traditional role as wife and mother, nor did she call anyone a chauvinist pig. The happiest period of Mary's own life was when

Mary Wollstonecraft is portrayed opposite as the inspiration, if not founder, of the feminist movement. At her knee are her daughters: Fanny, her first-born, and Mary Godwin, who (as Mary Shelley) would be famous as the creator of Dr. Frankenstein.

she was married and awaiting the birth of her second child. And the greatest delight she ever knew was in her first child, an illegitimate daughter. Mary's feminism may not appear today to be the hard-core revolutionary variety, but she did live, for a time, a scandalous and unconventional life— "emancipated," it is called by those who have never tried it. The essence of her thought, however, is simply that a woman's mind is as good as a man's.

Not many intelligent men could be found to dispute this proposition today, at least not in mixed company. In Mary's time, to speak of *anybody's* rights, let alone woman's rights, was a radical act. In England, as in other nations, "rights" were an entity belonging to the government. The common run of mankind had little access to what we now call "human rights." As an example of British justice in the late eighteenth century, the law cited two hundred different capital crimes, among them shoplifting. An accused man was not entitled to counsel. A child could be tried and hanged as soon as an adult. The right to vote existed, certainly, but because of unjust apportionment, it had come to

mean little. In the United States some of these abuses had been corrected— but the rights of man did not extend past the color bar and the masculine gender was intentional. In the land of Washington and Jefferson, as in the land of George III, human rights were a new idea and woman's rights were not even an issue.

In France, in 1792, a Revolution in the name of equality was in full course, and woman's rights had at least been alluded to. The Revolutionary government drew up plans for female education—to the age of eight. "The education of the women should always be relative to the men," Rousseau had written in *Emile*. "To please, to be useful to us, to make us love and esteem them, to educate us when young, and take care of us when grown up, to advise, to console us, to render our lives easy and agreeable: these are the duties of women at all times, and what they should be taught in their infancy." And, less prettily, "Women have, or ought to have, but little liberty."

Rousseau would have found little cause for complaint in eighteenth-century England. An Englishwoman had almost the same civil status as an American slave. Thomas Hardy, a hundred years hence, was to base a novel on the idea of a man casually selling his wife and daughter at public auction. Obviously this was not a common occurrence, but neither is it wholly implausible. In 1792, and later, a woman could not own property, nor keep any earned wages. All that she possessed belonged to her husband. She could not divorce him, but he could divorce her and take her children. There was no law to say she could not grow up illiterate or be beaten every day.

Such was the legal and moral climate in which Mary Wollstonecraft lived. She was born in London in the spring of 1759, the second child and first daughter of Edward Wollstonecraft, a prosperous weaver. Two more daughters and two more sons were eventually born into the family, making six children in all. Before they had all arrived, Mr. Wollstonecraft came into an inheritance and decided to move his family to the country and become a gentleman farmer. But this plan failed. His money dwindled, and he began drinking heavily. His wife turned into a terrified wraith whose only interest was her eldest son, Edward. Only he escaped the beatings and abuse that his father dealt out regularly to every other household member, from Mrs. Wollstonecraft to the family dog. As often happens in large and disordered families, the eldest sister had to assume the role of mother and scullery maid. Mary was a bright, strong child, determined not to be broken, and she undertook her task energetically, defying her father when he was violent and keeping her younger brothers and sisters in hand. Clearly, Mary held the household together, and in so doing forfeited her own childhood. This experience left her with an everlasting gloomy streak, and was a strong factor in making her a reformer.

At some point in Mary's childhood, another injustice was visited upon her, though so commonplace for the time that she can hardly have felt the sting.

Her elder brother was sent away to be educated, and the younger children were left to learn their letters as best they could. The family now frequently changed lodgings, but from her ninth to her fifteenth year Mary went to a day school, where she had the only formal training of her life. Fortunately, this included French and composition, and somewhere Mary learned to read critically and widely. These skills, together with her curiosity and determination, were really all she needed. The *Vindication* is in some parts long-winded, ill-punctuated, and simply full of hot air, but it is the work of a well-informed mind.

Feminists—and Mary would gladly have claimed the title—inevitably, even deservedly, get bad notices. The term calls up an image of relentless battle-axes: "thin college ladies with eye-glasses, no-nonsense features, mouths thin as bologna slicers, a babe in one arm, a hatchet in the other, grey eyes bright with balefire," as Norman Mailer feelingly envisions his antagonists in the Women's Liberation Movement. He has conjured up all the horrid elements: the lips with a cutting edge, the baby immaculately conceived (one is forced to conclude), the lethal weapon tightly clutched, the desiccating college degree, the joylessness. Hanging miasmally over the tableau is the suspicion of a deformed sexuality. Are these girls man-haters, or worse? Mary Wollstonecraft, as the first of her line, has had each of these scarlet letters (except the B.A.) stitched upon her bosom. Yet she conformed very little to the hateful stereotype. In at least one respect, however, she would have chilled Mailer's bones. Having spent her childhood as an adult, Mary reached the age of nineteen in a state of complete joylessness. She was later to quit the role, but for now she wore the garb of a martyr.

Her early twenties were spent in this elderly frame of mind. First she went out as companion to an old lady living at Bath, and was released from this servitude only by a call to nurse the

dying Mrs. Wollstonecraft. Then the family broke up entirely, though the younger sisters continued off and on to be dependent on Mary. The family of Mary's dearest friend, Fanny Blood, invited her to come and stay with them; the two girls made a small living doing sewing and handicrafts, and Mary dreamed of starting a primary school. Eventually, in a pleasant village called Newington Green, this plan materialized and prospered. But Fanny Blood in the meantime had married and moved to Lisbon. She wanted Mary to come and nurse her through the birth of her first child. Mary reached Lisbon just in time to see her friend die of childbed fever, and returned home just in time to find that her sisters, in whose care the flourishing little school had been left, had lost all but two pupils.

Mary made up her mind to die. "My constitution is impaired, I hope I shan't live long," she wrote to a friend in February, 1786. Under this almost habitual grief, however, Mary was gaining some new sense of herself. Newington Green, apart from offering her a brief success as a schoolmistress, had brought her some acquaintance in the world of letters, most important among them, Joseph Johnson, an intelligent and successful London publisher in search of new writers. Debt-ridden and penniless, Mary set aside her impaired constitution and wrote her first book, probably in the space of a week. Johnson bought it for ten guineas and published it. Called *Thoughts on the Education of Daughters*, it went unnoticed, and the ten guineas was soon spent. Mary had to find work. She accepted a position as governess in the house of Lord and Lady Kingsborough in the north of Ireland.

Mary's letters from Ireland to her sisters and to Joseph Johnson are so filled with Gothic gloom, so stained with tears, that one cannot keep from laughing at them. "I entered the great gates with the same kind of feeling I should have if I was going to the Bastille," she wrote upon entering Kingsborough Castle in the fall of 1786. Mary was now twenty-seven. Her most recent biographer, Margaret George, believes that Mary was not really suffering so much as she was having literary fantasies. In private she was furiously at work on a novel entitled, not very artfully, *Mary, A Fiction.* This is the story of a young lady of immense sensibilities who closely resembles Mary except that she has wealthy parents, a neglectful bridegroom, and an attractive lover. The title and fantasizing contents are precisely what a scribbler of thirteen might secretly concoct. Somehow Mary was embarking on her adolescence—with all its daydreams—fifteen years after the usual date. Mary's experience in Kingsborough Castle was a fruitful one, for all her complaints. In the summer of 1787 she lost her post as governess and set off for London with her novel. Not only did Johnson accept it for publication, he offered her a regular job as editor and translator and helped her find a place to live.

Thus, aged twenty-eight, Mary put aside her doleful persona as the martyred, set-upon elder sister. How different she is now, jauntily writing from London to her sisters: "Mr. Johnson . . . assures me that if I exert my talents in writing I may support myself in a comfortable way. I am then going to be the first of a new genus . . ." Now Mary discovered the sweetness of financial independence earned by interesting work. She had her own apartment. She was often invited to Mr. Johnson's dinner parties, usually as the only female guest among all the most interesting men in London: Joseph Priestley, Thomas Paine, Henry Fuseli, William Blake, Thomas Christie, William Godwin—all of them up-and-coming scientists or poets or painters or philosophers, bound together by left-wing political views. Moreover, Mary was successful in her own writing as well as in editorial work. Her *Original Stories for Children* went into three editions and was illustrated by Blake. Johnson and his friend Thomas

Christie had started a magazine called the *Analytical Review,* to which Mary became a regular contributor.

But—lest anyone imagine an elegantly dressed Mary presiding flirtatiously at Johnson's dinner table—her social accomplishments were rather behind her professional ones. Johnson's circle looked upon her as one of the boys. "Wollstonecraft" is what William Godwin calls her in his diary. One of her later detractors reported that she was at this time a "philosophic sloven," in a dreadful old dress and beaver hat, "with her hair hanging lank about her shoulders." Mary had yet to arrive at her final incarnation, but the new identity was imminent, if achieved by an odd route. Edmund Burke had recently published his *Reflections on the Revolution in France,* and the book had enraged Mary. The statesman who so readily supported the quest for liberty in the American colonies had his doubts about events in France.

Mary's reply to Burke, *A Vindication of the Rights of Men,* astounded London, partly because she was hitherto unknown, partly because it was good. Mary proved to be an excellent polemicist, and she had written in anger. She accused Burke, the erstwhile champion of liberty, of being "the champion of property." "Man preys on man," said she, "and you mourn for the idle tapestry that decorated a gothic pile and the dronish bell that summoned the fat priest to prayer." The book sold well. Mary moved into a better apartment and bought some pretty dresses—no farthingales, of course, but some of the revolutionary new "classical" gowns. She put her auburn hair up in a loose knot. Her days as a philosophic sloven were over.

Vindication of the Rights of Woman was her next work. In its current edition it runs to 250-odd pages; Mary wrote it in six weeks. *Vindication* is no prose masterpiece, but it has never failed to arouse its audience, in one

way or another. Horace Walpole unintentionally set the style for the book's foes. Writing to his friend Hannah More in August, 1792, he referred to Thomas Paine and to Mary as "philosophizing serpents" and was "glad to hear you have not read the tract of the last mentioned writer. I would not look at it." Neither would many another of Mary's assailants, the most virulent of whom, Ferdinand Lundberg, surfaced at the late date of 1947 with a tract of his own, *Modern Woman, the Lost Sex.* Savagely misogynistic as it is, this book was hailed in its time as "the best book yet to be written about women." Lundberg calls Mary the Karl Marx of the feminist movement, and the *Vindication* a "fateful book," to which "the tenets of feminism, which have undergone no change to our day, may be traced." Very well, but then, recounting Mary's life with the maximum possible number of errors per line, he warns us that she was "an extreme neurotic of a compulsive type" who "wanted to turn on men and injure them." In one respect, at least, Mr. Lundberg hits the mark: he blames Mary for starting women in the pernicious habit of wanting an education. In the nineteenth century, he relates, English and American feminists were hard at work. "Following Mary Wollstonecraft's prescription, they made a considerable point about acquiring a higher education." This is precisely Mary's prescription, and the most dangerous idea in her fateful book.

"Men complain and with reason, of the follies and caprices of our Sex," she writes in Chapter 1. "Behold, I should answer, the natural effect of ignorance." Women, she thinks, are usually so mindless as to be scarcely fit for their roles as wives and mothers. Nevertheless, she believes this state not to be part of the feminine nature, but the result of an equally mindless oppression, as demoralizing for men as for women. If a woman's basic mission is as a wife and mother, need she be an illiterate slave for this?

The heart of the work is Mary's attack on Rousseau. In *Emile* Rousseau had set forth some refreshing new ideas for the education of little boys. But women, he decreed, are tools for pleasure, creatures too base for moral or political or educational privilege. Mary recognized that this view was destined to shut half the human race out of all hope for political freedom. *Vindication* is a plea that the "rights of men" ought to mean the "rights of humanity." The human right that she held highest was the right to have a mind and think with it. Virginia Woolf, who lived through a time of feminist activity, thought that the *Vindication* was a work so true "as to seem to contain nothing new." Its originality, she wrote, rather too optimistically, had become a commonplace.

Vindication went quickly into a second edition. Mary's name was soon known all over Europe. But as she savored her fame—and she did savor it—she found that the edge was wearing off and that she was rather lonely. So far as anyone knows, Mary had reached this point in her life without ever having had a love affair. Johnson was the only man she was close to, and he was, as she wrote him, "A father, or a brother—you have been both to me." Mary was often now in the company of the Swiss painter Henry Fuseli, and suddenly she developed what she thought was a Platonic passion in his direction. He rebuffed her, and in the winter of 1792 she went to Paris, partly to escape her embarrassment but also because she wanted to observe the workings of the Revolution firsthand.

Soon after her arrival, as she collected notes for the history of the Revolution she hoped to write, Mary saw Louis XVI, "sitting in a hackney coach . . . going to meet death." Back in her room that evening, she wrote to Mr. Johnson of seeing "eyes glare through a glass door opposite my chair and bloody hands shook at me . . . I am going to bed and for the first time in my life, I cannot put out the candle." As the weeks went on, Edmund Burke's im-

placable critic began to lose her faith in the brave new world. "The aristocracy of birth is levelled to the ground, only to make room for that of riches," she wrote. By February France and England were at war, and British subjects classified as enemy aliens.

Though many Englishmen were arrested, Mary and a large English colony stayed on. One day in spring, some friends presented her to an attractive American, newly arrived in Paris, Gilbert Imlay. Probably about four years Mary's senior, Imlay, a former officer in the Continental Army, was an explorer and adventurer. He came to France seeking to finance a scheme for seizing Spanish lands in the Mississippi valley. This "natural and unaffected creature," as Mary was later to describe him, was probably the social lion of the moment, for he was also the author of a best-selling novel called *The Emigrants*, a farfetched account of life and love in the American wilderness. He and Mary soon became lovers. They were a seemingly perfect pair. Imlay must have been pleased with his famous catch, and—dear, liberated girl that she was—Mary did not insist upon marriage. Rather the contrary. But fearing that she was in danger as an Englishwoman, he registered her at the American embassy as his wife.

Blood was literally running in the Paris streets now, so Mary settled down by herself in a cottage at Neuilly. Imlay spent his days in town, working out various plans. The Mississippi expedition came to nothing, and he decided to stay in France and go into the import-export business, part of his imports being gunpowder and other war goods run from Scandinavia through the English blockade. In the evenings he would ride out to the cottage. By now it was summer, and Mary, who spent the days writing, would often stroll up the road to meet him, carrying a basket of freshly-gathered grapes.

A note she wrote Imlay that summer shows exactly what her feelings for him were: "You can scarcely imagine with what pleasure I anticipate the day when

we are to begin almost to live together; and you would smile to hear how many plans of employment I have in my head, now that I am confident that my heart has found peace . . ." Soon she was pregnant. She and Imlay moved into Paris. He promised to take her to America, where they would settle down on a farm and raise six children. But business called Imlay to Le Havre, and his stay lengthened ominously into weeks.

Imlay's letters to Mary have not survived, and without them it is hard to gauge what sort of man he was and what he really thought of his adoring mistress. Her biographers like to make him out a cad, a philistine, not half good enough for Mary. Perhaps; yet the two must have had something in common. His novel, unreadable though it is now, shows that he shared her political views, including her feminist ones. He may never have been serious about the farm in America, but he was a miserably long time deciding to leave Mary alone. Though they were seprated during the early months of her pregnancy, he finally did bring her to Le Havre, and continued to live with her there until the child was born and for some six months afterward. The baby arrived in May, 1794, a healthy little girl, whom Mary named Fanny after her old friend. Mary was proud that her delivery had been easy, and as for Fanny, Mary loved her instantly. "My little Girl," she wrote to a friend, "begins to suck so manfully that her father reckons saucily on her writing the second part of the Rights of Woman." Mary's joy in this child illuminates almost every letter she wrote henceforth.

Fanny's father was the chief recipient of these letters with all the details of the baby's life. To Mary's despair, she and Imlay hardly ever lived together again. A year went by; Imlay was now in London and Mary in France. She offered to break it off, but mysteriously, he could not let go. In the last bitter phase of their involvement, after she had joined him in London at his behest, he even sent her—as "Mrs. Imlay"—on a complicated business errand to the Scandinavian countries. Returning to London, Mary discovered that he was living with another woman. By now half crazy with humiliation, Mary chose a dark night and threw herself in the Thames. She was nearly dead when two rivermen pulled her from the water.

Though this desperate incident was almost the end of Mary, at least it was the end of the Imlay episode. He sent a doctor to care for her, but they rarely met again. Since Mary had no money, she set about providing for herself and Fanny in the way she knew. The faithful Johnson had already brought out Volume I of her history of the French Revolution. Now she set to work editing and revising her *Letters Written during a Short Residence in Sweden, Norway, and Denmark,* a kind of thoughtful travelogue. The book was well received and widely translated.

And it also revived the memory of Mary Wollstonecraft in the mind of an old acquaintance, William Godwin. As the author of the treatise *Political Justice,* he was now as famous a philosophizing serpent as Mary and was widely admired and hated as a "freethinker." He came to call on Mary. They became friends and then lovers. Early in 1797 Mary was again pregnant. William Godwin was an avowed atheist who had publicly denounced the very institution of marriage. On March 29, 1797, he nevertheless went peaceably to church with Mary and made her his wife.

The Godwins were happy together, however William's theories may have been outraged. He adored his small stepdaughter and took pride in his brilliant wife. Awaiting the birth of her child throughout the summer, Mary worked on a new novel and made plans for a book on "the management of infants"—it would have been the first "Dr. Spock." She expected to have another easy delivery and promised to come downstairs to dinner the day following. But when labor began, on August 30, it proved to be long and agonizing. A daughter, named Mary Wollstonecraft, was born; ten days later, the mother died.

Occasionally, when a gifted writer dies young, one can feel, as in the example of Shelley, that perhaps he had at any rate accomplished his best work. But so recently had Mary come into her full intellectual and emotional growth that her death at the age of thirty-eight is bleak indeed. There is no knowing what Mary might have accomplished now that she enjoyed domestic stability. Perhaps she might have achieved little or nothing further as a writer. But she might have been able to protect her daughters from some part of the sadness that overtook them; for as things turned out, both Fanny and Mary were to sacrifice themselves.

Fanny grew up to be a shy young girl, required to feel grateful for the roof over her head, overshadowed by her prettier half sister, Mary. Godwin in due course married a formidable widow named Mrs. Clairmont, who brought her own daughter into the house—the Claire Clairmont who grew up to become Byron's mistress and the mother of his daughter Allegra. Over the years Godwin turned into a hypocrite and a miser who nevertheless continued to pose as the great liberal of the day. Percy Bysshe Shelley, born the same year that the *Vindication of the Rights of Woman* was published, came to be a devoted admirer of Mary Wollstonecraft's writing. As a young man he therefore came with his wife to call upon Godwin. What he really sought, however, were Mary's daughters—because they were her daughters. First he approached Fanny, but later changed his mind. Mary Godwin was then sixteen, the perfect potential soul mate for a man whose needs for soul mates knew no bounds. They conducted their courtship in the most up-to-the-minute romantic style: beneath a tree near her mother's grave they read aloud to each other from the *Vindication.* Soon they eloped, having pledged their "troth" in the cemetery. Godwin, the celebrated freethinker, was enraged. To make matters worse, Claire Clairmont had run off to Switzerland with them.

Not long afterward Fanny, too, ran away. She went to an inn in a distant town and drank a fatal dose of laudanum. It has traditionally been said that unrequited love for Shelley drove her to this pass, but there is no evidence one way or the other. One suicide that can more justly be laid at Shelley's door is that of his first wife, which occurred a month after Fanny's and which at any rate left him free to wed his mistress, Mary Godwin. Wife or mistress, she had to endure poverty, ostracism, and Percy's constant infidelities. But now at last her father could, and did, boast to his relations that he was father-in-law to a baronet's son. "Oh, philosophy!" as Mary Godwin Shelley remarked.

If in practice Shelley was merely a womanizer, on paper he was a convinced feminist. He had learned this creed from Mary Wollstonecraft. Through his verse Mary's ideas began to be disseminated. They were one part of that vast tidal wave of political, social, and artistic revolution that arose in the late eighteenth century, the romantic movement. But because of Mary's unconventional way of life, her name fell into disrepute during the nineteenth century, and her book failed to exert its rightful influence on the development of feminism. Emma Willard and other pioneers of the early Victorian period indignantly refused to claim Mary as their forebear. Elizabeth Cady Stanton and Lucretia Mott were mercifully less strait-laced on the subject. In 1889, when Mrs. Stanton and Susan B. Anthony published their *History of Woman Suffrage,* they dedicated the book to Mary. Though Mary Wollstonecraft can in no sense be said to have founded the woman's rights movement, she was, by the late nineteenth century, recognized as its inspiration, and the *Vindication* was vindicated for the highly original work it was, a landmark in the history of society.

The Drunken Organ Repairman
Easter, 1968

When the church was built it was built into it.
My blood into my neck; forehead to scalp;
blow of my heel on the pavement to my elbow;
rise of a hill to the stick pushing to the summit.

On the first Sunday in Lent when the organmaster
pulled the great manual from the oaken bank,
alarums—beetles and spiders falling through iron—
slid down the walls and stirred the flowerets
on the ladies' hats who had come to take pleasure of the Lord.

It had been in the ribs two hundred years.
When a hymnal fell to the floor or a child wailed
when the holy oils slid up its nose, the organ
spat a low hustle through the air. Death drew
a gray wind from the grill and snuffed
the candles stuck into the coffin lid.

He came from Maine, with a satchel of wrenches
and tuning forks, three cases of gin, a camping bed,
two lanterns, a mending torch, a can of oil and broke
it down to the nails and clamps that hold the pipes
and keys to the magnets in the pith; he spilt
oil upon them like a rain god until it seemed
they breathed.

       It took a year to cure the spasm
in the pipes. The smell of gin, oil, fire, and gas,
like a motor over a mechanic pit, hung in the nave
until Pentecost when he sprinkled gin in the center
of the pumps and bellows and walked out the Church
toward Maine.

       The organmaster pulled the great manual
from the oaken bank and alarums of the Paraclete—
fields of violets, stone fences, honey bees, wrens
in the barns, crashed against the white buds and
split the green wood in the apple trees.

By NED O'GORMAN